Awakening the Third Eye

Discovering the True Essence of Recapitulation

Lujan Matus

Disclaimer

All rights reserved. No part of this publication may be reproduced or transferred in any form or by any means, graphic, electronic, or mechanical, including photocopying, recording, taping, or by any information storage retrieval system, without the written permission of the author. The author specifically disclaims any responsibility for any liability, loss, or risk, personal or otherwise, which is incurred as a consequence, directly or indirectly, of the use and application of any of the contents of this book.

© Copyright 2010 Lujan Matus.
The Parallel Perception logo is copyright.
No unauthorized use.

ISBN-10: 1453651837
ISBN-13: 978-1453651834

Dedication

To my dear friends,

Thank you for your loving and unconditional support.

Deep appreciation to Lyra for the internal graphic images.

With deepest gratitude to my beloved wife,

Mizpah Matus.

Acknowledgements

Cover art by Grinning Tree.

Editing, formatting, cover design layout and back cover synopsis by Naomi Jean.

Table of Contents

Preface I

THE RESPONSIBILITY OF THE NAGUAL 1
Universal Light Fibers 7
The Gateless Way 13

WHISPERING OF THE NAGUAL 19

SEEKING ALIGNMENT 68
The Dream Walker 71
Empathic Dreaming 76

THE TECHNIQUES, SERIES ONE: UNVEILING THE THIRD EYE 106
Technique 1: *The Mirror* 107
Technique 2: *Dragon's Breath* 112
Technique 3: Stargazing one: *Eternity's Gaze*
Recapitulation Preparation 113
Eternity's Gaze Illustration 117

Losing the Need for Validation 118
Plant Gazing Preparation 121
Technique 4: *Gazing At One Plant* 123
Gazing At One Plant Illustration 127
Technique 5: *Gazing At Two Plants* 128
Gazing at Two Plants illustration 132
Walking the Gaze In 133
Always Rotate Clockwise.. 134
Technique 6: Stargazing two: *Seeing Light Fibers*................. 145
Technique 7: *People Gazing*... 147
Technique 8: *Equalization: Turning off the Right Eye*........ 153
Equalization A illustration 157
Equalization B illustration 158
The Swastikas and the Eyes of the Seer.................................... 159
Swastikas and the Eyes of the Seer illustration 165
Technique 9: *Third Eye Awakening Meditation*...................... 168
Technique 10: *Ascension and Descension* 171
Ascension and Descension illustration 174
Technique 11: *Meditation to Accompany the Ascension and Descension* 184

HARVESTING AND SKIMMING ETERNITY. 189

THE TECHNIQUES, SERIES TWO: ADVANCED GAZING 206

Technique 12: *Gateway*..208
Gateway Illustration 212
Technique 13: *Moon Gazing*..213
Quetzalcoatl Moon Gazing A illustration 216

QUETZALCOATL MOON GAZING B ILLUSTRATION 217
TECHNIQUE 14: *LIGHTNING GAZING* 219
TECHNIQUE 15: *BONE MARROW BREATHING* 222

THE ACTIVE DREAMER 225

DÉJÀ VU, PREMONITIONS AND OMENS 252
TECHNIQUE 16: *FLOWER GAZING ONE* 256
TECHNIQUE 17: *FLOWER GAZING TWO* 266
TECHNIQUE 18: *RAINBOW GAZING* 268
EPILOGUE 271

Preface

Awakening the Third Eye is an account of Lujan Matus' personal journey, described as an unraveling mystery even to himself, and offered as a context for the extraordinary information he imparts. His teachings take the form of techniques - both precise and abstract in nature - and insights, whose relevance formulate in the circumstances surrounding the reader, as you will discover for yourself.

Lujan's writing is very direct and at the same time multi-layered. Switching between styles – conversational, storytelling, instructional, raw and poetic – he has a densely faceted flow

PREFACE

that appears in the moment and is documented exactly as it arrives. Amongst other things, this approach provokes a multi-lateral assimilation that challenges the linear process we habitually adopt in regard to just about everything we do.

Awakening the Third Eye is a unique and auspicious work, illuminating a subject veiled in timeless mystery. In the thoroughly globalized context we now find ourselves in, it seems unlikely that anything truly revelatory could possibly be introduced that is not already available *somewhere* out there.

In these writings you will recognize that rare quality of originality in both senses of the word; that is, *innovative or previously unseen,* and, *originating from source.*

Whatever you have already read, heard or learnt relating to the third eye, whether from ancient manuscripts, articles documenting the latest quantum research or anywhere else within the great pool of traditional and contemporary knowledge now at our fingertips; what is conveyed here is something else. It is a perspective we need to come to terms with, which essentially addresses how to access this precious wisdom within

PREFACE

ourselves.

A profound acknowledgment takes place internally as we absorb Lujan's experiences in this and other realities. The confirmation effect is intense, jolting us with immediacy. What he shares is simultaneously revelatory in regard to our conditioned state of being and deeply recognizable to the universal consciousness that resides within each of us.

Through traversing these incredible elucidations we are drawn in to access our own strange and unfathomable nature. Specifically, we are intimately reacquainted with our mysterious dimensionality and how we can comprehend it in the moment that it reveals itself to us.

Third eye perception is much more than an esoteric preoccupation. It is our link to source, to eternity, and to unity. This capacity represents access to timeless knowing that passes through our very cells and is delivered directly into present consciousness, when we know how to listen. What could be more relevant and valuable right now?

PREFACE

All that we have lost through severance from that innate unity is all that we need to recover in order to transform our current trajectory of destructive ignorance and selfish preoccupation into a living approach that is full of wisdom and cooperation of the highest order.

Reconnecting to third eye awareness brings us into a realm of experience where our universal bond becomes so apparent that to act against our higher nature is fundamentally counterproductive in a practical and tangible sense.

Inevitably priorities are transformed when our choices are viewed from the greater context of being witnessed by ourselves from all eternity, a perspective we are reacquainted with within these pages.

As conscious beings we have much to contend with and there is no shortcut through the complexities that face each of us. All we can do is follow our insights, cultivate our own integrity and make a moment to moment choice to be real, based on indications from our heart center.

www.parallelperception.com

PREFACE

To be provided with keys and directly applicable techniques that realign us with this purpose and help us develop the power of our intuitive independence is an inestimable gift.

With language itself reflecting the limitations of our current evolutionary state, it is no easy feat to communicate about that which dwells outside of parameters that have long been established.

I am elated when I come across words with the power to deliver me into the wordless, and Lujan's works have a unique capacity to directly catalyze this precious experience. He has a way of weaving and directing awareness beyond syntactical and cognitive barriers, providing an open mind with an opportunity to travel into its own multi-dimensionality, a truly profound realm that we instantly understand should never have been forsaken.

These reminders, examples and techniques are priceless. We are so saturated with the known, with linear descriptions, rational premises and a clinging attachment to the borders of our certainty that our greater self has learnt to be less than what it is in order to accommodate the limitations we have been conditioned to accept.

If only we could be who we really are. If only we could remember our wholeness. By teaching ourselves how to listen to the part of us that knows, we can. In order to do this we first have to break the hypnotic hold our construct has on us or, perhaps more precisely, that we have on it.

Presentation has come to dominate our reality - through narrative, visual stimulus or the triggering of our other senses - capturing our attention and diverting our stream of consciousness into avenues of awareness that are dangerously absorbing and often false.

It is no wonder that we struggle to access our center and find ourselves caught up in intricacies that appear to be endless, not knowing where to locate truth amidst these relentless onslaughts. Yet, as the perceiver, we nevertheless have a responsibility to understand and own our part in this process.

This is exactly why the information contained in this book is important. It offers a means to help decipher, navigate and

PREFACE

ultimately disentangle ourselves from the fetters of a socialized perspective.

Our third eye perception cannot be deceived in the way our habitual awareness can be. The messages we receive from this mystic capacity, though veiled, have the power to lead us out of distorted consciousness and onto the path we are meant to walk.

This exquisite facility to know truth, to see what is not apparent, and to receive messages from the unknown, is part of us. We are multi-dimensional perceptor-creators endowed with an impersonal intelligence that links us to all that is, all that was and all that can be.

Our very DNA contains the light encoded wisdom that is our heritage and represents the physical manifestation of our inevitable state of union with all that is. Remembering this is crucial to our evolution.

We have become so absorbed in the segmentation that allows us to process the vastness in our capacity as individuals that the very proposition of unity and universal consciousness appears

www.parallelperception.com

PREFACE

to many to be a kind of utopian science fiction that bears no relationship with reality.

Nevertheless, whether we understand it or not, whether we accept or reject such concepts, and however we choose to name the phenomenon, we have all experienced our universal link in one way or another. It is who we are and we cannot avoid it.

I would prefer not to label such experiences as *spiritual*, *metaphysical* or *supernatural*, for it can be counter-productive to isolate what is so primordial through overly connoted definitions.

To put it simply, our third eye connectivity is intrinsic to our personal and communal experience, and we need to leave room for that particular awareness to enter into our daily lives.

I am eternally grateful for the contribution Lujan Matus is making to global consciousness through touching individuals with his writings, and through the generous and impeccable sincerity of his example. He is a person truly living within his own integrity, which is an invaluable stance in that it makes this very quality less rare in the world, inspiring others to dare to take the path of

PREFACE

authenticity in their own way.

The result of Lujan's personal application to what presented itself to him as both his responsibility and his gift is that he has been able to travel deeply into our galactic nature and return to share the secrets absorbed on his journey.

I hope that the seeds of this precious stardust will flower in your vision and that through this new gaze upon the world you will forge a reality that allows the pure expression of your spirit to blossom and grow.

Naomi Jean.

www.parallelperception.com

THE RESPONSIBILITY
OF THE NAGUAL

A nagual is a bearer of altered perceptions that are passed down orally or transmitted interdimensionally, either through dreaming or in lucid pre-cognitive states. The responsibility of a nagual is to harvest, act upon and communicate the echoes of eternity that are conveyed to them through their third eye seeing.

Third eye perception is within everyone's capabilities. Some people are born with the resources to operate that perceptual capacity with two or three hundred energy compartments. Other individuals are fortunate enough to have four hundred energy compartments and these individuals are known as naguals.

A nagual's responsibility is to supply the initial impetus that allows realizations to be imparted, and thus realized, through envisioning the inconceivable. This capacity is utilized as an expansive net that traverses the known and the unknown, eternally skimming from a central matrix that returns to itself in singular multiples that become the whisperings of spirit.

To use the symbology of numbers to describe the scope of this, if we have four hundred elements that can be endlessly combined in different arrangements, the potential represented is colossal.

With two or three hundred compartments the possible combinations of these elements are also so great as to be practically limitless. Nevertheless, the initial impetus of the nagual is required to break the bounds of the known, enabling others to traverse that limitlessness within the capacity of their own personal configurations.

By virtue of having a womb, women have an extraordinary ability to traverse within the vast boundaries of precognitive awareness. The reason this is the case is that the womb has access to the perceptual net of that which is to be created.

Thus the capacity of another individual's third eye awareness is combined with and thereby utilized by that of the woman, even before the child is born.

The capacity of the womb as a sensory organ has the ability to draw upon the incalculable equation that is the unknown, which is limitlessness itself. The womb can access this limitlessness as a primary boost for precognitive awareness, even if the woman is childless.

The only drawback of this is that women may fall into a deeper state of morbid emotionality, thus forgoing the levity to access the vibratory elements that govern the heart's primary function; as a conduit and impetus to communicate unencumbered by the original morbidity which causes a controlling factor to come into play.

This function that appears to be aware of everything that occurs simultaneously, not only for a female but also for a male nagual, affects both similarly.

In essence, it is vitally important for each to reach a state of controlled folly - which is a formlessness that does not attach itself to the outcomes of circumstances, yet is fully cognizant of what is occurring - before they fall into the depths that are the intricacies of what they see, so as not to become lost to the never ending loop known as the art of stalking; which is hunting or tracking the elements of somebody else's reality for self gratification.

Immersion in these kinds of behavioral modes requires one to rigidly adhere to the factors that appear as a circumstantial platform that guides the perception of the seer. Many lineages have been lost within the labyrinthine constructs of such principles.

Therefore the art of controlled folly - seeking the seer within and not searching for pursuing selfish ends - must be re-encountered, to free humanity from absorption in the attention required to stalk, so that we may lose our identity and become of service to that which can only be known at the moment that it presents itself.

As we progressively practice the art of controlled folly our containment will be confronted by limitlessness itself. Encountering the unknown stretches the limits of any being's perception, no matter how fluid they are or how much energy is at their disposal. To face eternity from a mortal perspective demands an elasticity that goes far beyond normal perception, and this is where the third eye comes in.

It must be understood that the third eye is veiled by nature. This veiling filters the complex influx of information coming from past, present and future events which inevitably define the adaptivity of the path that the seer walks upon.

Within the perceptual net of the third eye is a pre-ordained force that emanates back to the seer. By virtue of this receptivity they do the bidding of the heart, which outlines the path that they must walk upon.

If by chance the seer does not wait in a state of absolute fortitude that bears witness to the oncoming complexities of that which presents itself, and speaks beyond the boundaries of their impeccability, then what they patiently await will not arrive.

Thus thrown out of the elusive state of non-interference, the world begins and the touch of eternity ends for the one who calculates within the restrictive boundaries of the social milieu.

In this case the net that is thrown adjusts and becomes a boundless calculability that can find no peace. It is imperative to touch lightly that which leaves its impressionless image upon one's consciousness.

Universal Light Fibers

Whilst absorbed in a deep state of meditation, I was viewing the world from an elevated perspective, far out in space, when suddenly I found myself ushered behind the reality I witnessed. I was swiftly confronted by innumerable strands of light filaments that were self conscious and appeared to be randomly opportunistic by nature.

At the point of interaction I became aware that within their configuration they respond to the available consciousness presented, utilizing the will of the host to manifest the construct that corresponds to the reflections and limitations of that awareness, whether organic or inorganic by nature.

Once the filaments recognized that I was noticing them, I got somehow flung behind them. I then found myself in absolute blackness with no stars. This was an unfathomable darkness, dense with information, yet reflecting nothing. The containment of any sort of identity was impossible. Any shred of individuality, even as a witness, could not withstand this place.

Absorbing what presented itself at that point, I realized that I was being viewed by millions upon millions of eyes that conveyed to me that I was not the only perceiver. As the crushing force of this realization pushed upon my being, I conceived that I was observing myself from multiple perspectives.

As the eyes pressed upon me they seemed to be demanding to know what I was doing there, where no such consciousness could normally arrive. The isolation of being observed in this way was unbearable in terms of the endless longing that was presented.

What I was perceiving was my third eye capacity, universally witnessed. It was apparent at that point that I was not the singular entity that I expected to discover; yet the perception that I encountered *was* myself, within dimension. I was very fortunate to survive this encounter. I became aware that I should not have been able to cope with being viewed from this perspective.

The pressure applied was so intense that my single being, which was being perceived by myself in multiples, could have exploded into light and perhaps continued on another journey, or that the journey could have ended at that point.

I have no way of knowing. To speculate is foolish. What did happen is that I was thrown back into the living construct. Other seers have described this experience as *jumping into the abyss.*

I realized at that point that each living construct created via consciousness is only familiar with the corresponding light filaments that allow that particular energetic configuration to manifest what actually *can* be known as a consequence of what exists within those bands of awareness. At any level the rule applies, that the construct will correspond to the relative grid of that consciousness.

In order to expand individually and collectively, communal

conductivity is where we need to direct our awareness. This conductivity demands that each knows what has already been universally organized and submits to what is presented and does not dictate through individual desire - yet individual desire governs the dictums of awareness, for the bidding becomes the true expression of one's individuality.

By virtue of the fact that we are going to come into existence, that we are going to be born, our third eye capacity interlinks with the universe at large and the unknown already knows what is going to be known.

For example, if a seer is to traverse the vastness of the unknowable, their fragile being will disintegrate into fragments that will inevitably turn to look back upon what had originally existed within the limited time frame of that lifespan.

Upon that point of seeing what was, they will be irreversibly absorbed into what is, as if they never existed. Thus the nature of the universe is revealed. Through this unveiling, if a seer survives such an encounter, they will harvest fragments of the unknowable into whispers of wisdom, to be later accessed as ineffable memories, which gives the inconceivable the possibility to be envisioned.

The light filaments are the energetic units that hold our construct intact, that form our living world. They interact by virtue of our wants and desires.

This becomes our capacity to influence the structure of reality through the fractal effect of the incalculable force of our third eye capacity to expand beyond our wildest expectations via the fact that it is eternally connected to an unknown factor, which conversely is also influenced by our socially determined limitations.

This interactivity is precisely why constructs in their myriad manifestations are so absorbing, no matter how expansive, and why desire-based systems are self-delineating. For they will perpetually turn inwards, reflecting only upon what is known and not going beyond the gratification of the wants and perceived needs of that awareness.

We are witnessing ourselves

from all time.

Our thoughts and actions echo

throughout eternity;

They are noted

and duly reflected back

upon ourselves.

The Gateless Way

The way conforms, yet it is non-conformity itself. It speaks, yet the voice that is spoken does not belong to the seer. The seer witnesses the emerging wisdom as a gift and inherent surprise that travels upon the imagery presented, which transforms into words whose very impetus has arrived from the unknown to be communicated via the medium that is the pressure of the one who inquires. Without the inquiry, one cannot speak and convey what one knows.

We are intimately interconnected, evolutionarily bound, like an endless knot. This is how the oral tradition continues from nagual to nagual, from nagual to disciple, invariably transforming in comparison to the receiving consciousness.

Even though each nagual's transmission varies, it compounds and builds upon what previously existed, naturally distilling only what is necessary, thereby transforming what was into what will be, re-establishing expansive parameters beyond, yet combining with, what was previously known.

The empaths heart is compelled to walk upon the words that are conveyed through the pressure relayed. A seer will only speak of what is seen, not of what they know. The validation of knowing is irrelevant in comparison to what is presented in the circumstance.

If no words are to be spoken there is an instantaneous realization between the witness and the recipient acting only upon the wordless, thus giving steps to the unknown in a tangible world. A warrior's steps are traceless impressions that only last for a moment.

Once the gravity of this momentary threshold is reached then the tangibility of what *was* disappears into what *is,* and the universal fractalization awaits to reappear - in correspondence to the power of the individual - to give substance to what will be.

The way appears as an image projected, which defines the internal pressure that applies itself as the voice that gives recognition to what is usually not recognized.

As a humanity, our legacy contains us within the limited parameters of its expectations. We are taught to see a solid world that reflects our reality. We then learn to speak. When we are spoken to our voice emerges in its purity, from childhood, but then unfortunately learns to speak to itself through the repetitious loops that are the complex socialization that surrounds this child.

Instead of having access to that imagery that appears externally as a childhood imagination, this facility is then turned inwardly as a narcissistic, self-reflective component that sustains a repetitive narrative and views only what has occurred, thus perpetuating what has been looked upon.

The voice that we once heard, that whispered to us, is turned inward to confer with the phantom consciousness that we invariably inherit. Coupled with dysfunctional emotions, this is the legacy that we have so easily accepted as our way.

Within our childhood purity we are transported to what we become, as a collective. However, it is the fully-grown human being I wish to speak to here. Be aware that you may be lost to your true self and the inherent power that lies therewithin.

Through the ancient techniques in this book you can finally discover the way that once was, that has been lost, so that we can all once again commence our journey of seeing collectively.

What I am saying here is that all of the imagery that is internal, we must allow to externalize itself, and not possess the images that appear inwardly, for they do not belong to us. They belong to the final command of our inevitability, our death. This very conclusion will view the images in the same way that has been described.

Our inevitability will take what was and show you who you were, and this ultimate traversing within itself is devastating. One is gripped by the eternal longing that is the seeing that we have missed on our journey, only confronted by our doings, the labor of our discontent in terms of not applying ourselves correctly to the living circumstance that presents itself.

However, magical thresholds are *always* appearing, which leave a tangible effect upon our being, giving the impression of traveling upon a path that has become pathless. To achieve this formless purpose we must forgo the control of attempting to possess our internal pictorial imagery and allow it to become the command of eternity.

This is true seeing, which appears as if projected from nowhere. Then one sees as we used to as children, but this receptivity re-manifests as the mature actualization of this numinous facility. Invariably the imagery that arrives will be absorbed as nuggets of information, which will dictate the directives and knowings of a pure heart that awaits what is meant to be instead of what one thinks should be.

To reach this magical threshold one must endeavor not to talk to oneself and silence the mind that speaks to a base of emotion that justifies its ends to its means. Yet we all know that it is not the means to the end that we are meant to traverse.

Once this simple but complex task is arrived upon, then it is advantageous for those who have learnt not to speak to themselves to then command themselves not to dream. Then the power of these images can be reassembled into the external imagery that will become the way: our third eye visionary capacity.

In some shamanic circles, the waking world is depicted as the first attention and the world of dreams is noted as the second attention. This is our heritage, our legacy: what we are and what we dream. The techniques in this book will invariably change this fixation, so that mankind can step delicately into what is known as the third attention: a slipstream of magic that is invariably guided by the dictums of eternity.

On this tenuous thread the way of the modern seer is now being revealed, yet these revelations have only transmitted what was already known. Thus a teacher is a conduit, giving the tools of independence to those who seek what they have forgotten, a reminder of the energetic medium that gives substance to the gateless way, which is found through acknowledgement of that which previously could not be seen.

WHISPERING OF THE NAGUAL

Over the course of this book being written certain students were invited to read the excerpts as they took form, giving rise to some very interesting questions and answers, which became this chapter.

Q: How can we as emerging seers verify the state of the hive or honeycombed capacity (the two, three or four hundred compartments) of our third eye perspective? Is it important to try to become aware of this structure?

A: As one emerges, they begin to see. I was fortunate enough to witness this capacity within myself. It was a byproduct of being in contact with my benefactor. I saw him manipulate this honeycomb maze so as to rearrange my capacity as a seer. I have never heard of this ever being done before but this doesn't necessarily mean it hasn't happened.

I have given a description above where through my own power I was confronted with that capacity, through seeing endless amounts of eyes viewing me from incalculable positions. When one sees one automatically knows what they see.

One immediately recognizes the number that is contained. It is simply the rule. Yet the rule does not govern the capacity - the innate abilities of each individual - whether they have four, three or two hundred compartments at their disposal. It is the very power of the warrior that determines their elasticity in terms of working with the combined forces of this particular facility that defines their life path.

Once warriors conceive of the incalculable combinations, they move appropriately towards their predetermined destination, and this will take into consideration any pitfalls and mistakes they make along their way, which cannot be seen as such if the trials and tribulations deliver them to the pinnacle that determines their fate.

I will say that there is an advantage to having a nagual's capacity. But this capacity within itself will only yield in comparison to one's ability to be steadfast in their absoluteness to succeed unbendingly.

Q: You say, "Nevertheless, the initial impetus of the nagual is required to break the bounds of the known, enabling others to traverse that limitlessness within the capacity of their personal configurations."

Does this mean that contact with the body of knowledge put forth by the nagual is sufficient? Or is direct contact required?

A: It is always advantageous to have direct contact. It is also advantageous to believe in oneself. A nagual gives the impetus to take away doubt, by virtue of the fact that they trust their seeing. They cut through the veil with absolute precision in comparison to each individual they meet.

Nevertheless, the body of knowledge that I am imparting

here gives a warrior the tools to initiate a cascade. I have been given many tools by my benefactor, and these very techniques I am passing on to those who have the inclination to fight for their freedom on an individual basis.

Q: "What I am saying here is that all of the imagery that is internal, we must allow to externalize itself."

What is the hallmark of this transition? Does it have a recognizable distinction from internal imagery? In other words, will we know it when it occurs?

A: Yes, it is recognized immediately when it occurs. When a warrior begins to see, imagery appears outside of themselves to be viewed for a split second. Contained within this image will be information that pertains to the present circumstance, or it may be precognitive in nature. One always knows when they see. Thus it is important to know what one is waiting for.

Q: "Third eye perception is within everyone's capabilities. Some people are born with the capacity to operate that perceptual net with two or three hundred energy compartments. Other individuals are fortunate enough to have four hundred energy compartments and these individuals are known as naguals. A nagual's responsibility is to supply the initial impetus that allows realizations to be imparted and thus realized, through envisioning the inconceivable."

Is it important to verify one's configuration with respect to one's capabilities? A nagual knows that he or she is a nagual because they were informed as such by another nagual... Is this correct?

How does this recognition take place? In the same vein, is it important for those of us who are not naguals to be recognized for what we offer in terms of our individual capabilities by another who can see these configurations?

A: A nagual identifying another nagual is a simple affair. When in each other's presence there is a comfort and fulfillment; a bolstering effect, and then if eternity deems appropriate the veil of the third eye will be released and the old will see the new in light of who they really are.

Even though this does not really identify how it occurs, I myself have found other naguals. One day when the veil is lifted, for those of you who know me, you will see me. The seeing will reveal in comparison to your capacity and you will know with absolute certainty.

It has been deemed important previously that all configurations are noted and categorized. This is not a primary focus any more. Categorizations lead to identification. It is now only important to enlist the available energy and thereby, if one is a nagual, to be immersed in the unknown, losing one's identity.

Only if that identity is lost can one truly lead. That is why it is of primary importance not to give credence to that which built a rule that dominated by establishing fixed boundaries. It is these very boundaries that must be eliminated.

The excess energy of a nagual will identify the prime directive. Once the prime directive is known, then it is up to each individual to live within their own boundaries of impeccability and within this integrity, a nagual does not seek to rule.

Q: "We are witnessing ourselves from all time. Our thoughts and actions echo throughout eternity; they are noted and duly reflected back upon ourselves."

I can't even conceive of what this means. Is it even important to try? Or is it something to simply accept as what will be revealed upon persisting in a state of controlled folly?

In other words, is controlled folly my only task for evolution in this world? Or should I meditate on the experiences of expanded boundaries of another's knowing in order to bring them about for myself?

A: Your experiences will reveal your path. What you await has already appeared. Each person's journey will vary as each tree of a different species bears different fruits. As one's consciousness is inclined so its season will culminate in the fruit of its experience.

Q: "Through the ancient techniques in this book you can finally discover the way that used to be, that has been lost, so that we can all once again commence our journey of seeing collectively"

I'm having a hard time allowing the notion of the need for controlled folly and the need for the practice of techniques to coexist. How can they? Isn't it enough to simply abandon oneself to a perennial state of controlled folly?

Why do we need seemingly ritualized practices of ancient techniques in order to become seated in this state which opens us to everything that is needed for us as it presents itself?

It seems like something ancient is stalking its persistence for its own purposes of existence beyond the natural confines of what presented itself for it. Of course, this is speculation. But still, the question is here. And thank you for the freedom to ask it.

A: Yes, you are right to inquire. The question is necessary. Once these methods are applied they seal the eyes in very much the same way that the eyes have been sealed and programmed with the realities that have been constructed that we are conscious of at the moment. Is it not the rituals of the present-day consciousness that confine us?

I have been given techniques that are tools; practices that

enliven the chakras from the heart center to the crown, bypassing the solar plexus, thereby disallowing descension into the lower regions. And here we should not kid ourselves about the lower regions.

We act upon one another as if the primary motive is more valuable than the life force lost. To falter and fall from our own grace is so common that is has been accepted as the foregone conclusion of our legacy.

Making a stand and speaking one's true voice is the most uncommon factor in the world at the moment, and historically we can see that those who have spoken beyond the social confines, in the most dramatic scenarios have been assassinated. This is the world that presently persists.

Nevertheless, to answer your question clearly and succinctly, once these practices fortify the eyes and the blue spectrum is identified, the warrior's seeing will gather its own momentum and what will occur will be a deprogramming of that which is known, unveiling new thresholds.

Once these limits are realized then the limitlessness of eternity - the third eye capacity - takes over, thereby rendering the techniques I have given obsolete and it is here that the true journey of the warrior commences, unencumbered by any ritualized practice.

Q: "Other individuals are fortunate enough to have four hundred energy compartments... eternally skimming from a central matrix that returns to itself in singular multiples that become the whisperings of spirit."

What exactly are these energy compartments? It seems here that they serve as little *scoops* that go out into the world gathering info from past, present and future. Do we then use these compartments to arrange our reality or attention? Are they filtered by the third eye and then the information contained within becomes seeing?

A: This is a very difficult question to answer. The third eye has a universal aspect. Its basic influence is governed from a primordial basis - *the beginning* - from the culmination of that to *the end* in terms of the far-reaching effect of its combined expansiveness to reach all spectrums that are essentially governed by one's personal power.

Each eye is filtered, for if they weren't the influx of information would be overwhelming; plus the traversing of a warrior is a journey of discovery. The veil gives significance to the fact that we are unified yet unsubstantiated all at once, for if we were not limited we would expand into our limitlessness.

Q: "The light filaments are the energetic units that hold our construct intact, which form our living world. They interact by virtue of our wants and desires and this becomes our capacity to influence the structure of reality..."

Are you describing the force of intent here? Is it intent that the filaments of light need, to be directed to create that which we intend..."our living world"?

A: Yes it is intent that I am describing here; a symbiotic, connective process. It may seem that there is a time delay between the filaments of light in correspondence to the desire. What you must realize is that even if the desire is not fulfilled the intention has its corresponding effect. Sometimes you get what you want; sometimes you get what you need.

Q: You describe the connection of the woman's womb to the possibility to create an additional third eye awareness giving her an advantage. What if a woman has had a hysterectomy (surgical removal of the organ)? Will she lose that advantage?

A: While the womb is functioning the third eye capacity will expand and contract within its seemingly limited time frame, yet the time frame that it expanded upon is limitless. What may appear negative is only that way via perceiving the limitation as such.

Q: "It must be explained that the third eye is veiled by nature. This veiling filters the complex influx of information coming from past, present and future events which inevitably define the adaptivity of the path that the seer walks upon. Within this perceptual net is a pre-ordained force that emanates back to the seer. By virtue of this they do the bidding of the heart, which outlines the path that they must walk."

"To achieve this we must forgo the control of attempting to possess our internal pictorial imagery and allow it to become the command of eternity. This is true seeing, which appears as if projected from nowhere."

"Invariably this imagery will be absorbed as nuggets of information that will dictate the directives and knowings of a pure heart..."

From my understanding, the third eye also has the capacity to show us what another is seeing in their mind's eye, which can become confusing to a seer when the parties involved are not resolved, resulting in the projected imagery being interpreted as content arriving from that pre-ordained force. Is this why it is crucial to be in a state of controlled folly?

A: When one sees the internal pictorial imagery of another there is never confusion. The third eye is precise in its seeing. What can become confusing is that if this first type of seeing, which is internal, is then coupled with the harbored emotionality of the individual that has become aware, then doubt may arise from unresolved feelings that interfere with the seeing itself.

That is why it is so very important for a seer to go beyond this type of awareness. There are two types. The first is as you describe above, when the imagery is seen internally. The second type is when the imagery is seen externally.

The first instance is where seers learn to remember the items of their seeing and solicit their third eye aspect forcefully to acquiesce to their bent of nature, to intend an outcome that has to do with the fulfillment of their own desires.

Whether the conceptual body of knowledge of this seer is unreasonable or not makes no difference. They are simply using the black arts and will employ any means at their disposal to manipulate the circumstances to trigger responses, thereby educating themselves through the reactivity of the various individuals around them that they seek to control.

Covert activity is rife in the world at the moment and there is great confusion surrounding this first state of seeing. Some have more abilities than others, thus the perpetual cycle of dominance occurs. The primary components utilized within individuals like this are shame, blame and guilt, to establish the compliance necessary to hold the recipient in an iron grip of the protagonist's making.

This type of seeing, this first stage, can also be an auspicious step towards the latter. In many disciplines rules of conduct are outlined so as to guide the initiate away from the dark arts, waiting for the auspicious moment when their seeing becomes external and thus a new frontier opens.

For this to occur, one's internal dialog must be switched off completely. Obviously you will still be able to do mathematics and everything else that is necessary. This facility will be at the command of the seer. The internal pictorial imagery is then intended to be switched off as well, so as to bring the complex catacombs of dreaming streaming back into the third eye to be utilized by eternity.

At this point the initiate also intends for the dreams which appear in sleep to cease, so as to further empower the third eye capacity to be utilized in the waking world - as an inorganic essential element rooted in the living construct - instead of employed inorganically in an inorganic realm. This will empower the double or the dreaming body to station itself centrally within the physical body.

At this stage the initiate is given specific exercises to draw the external energetic field of the chakras so close that when they are active they can be physically felt spinning, as if there is a plate underneath the skin.

With this primordial intent that awakens the chakras to the world at large, the culmination of what one becomes aware of is the voice that the heart speaks, when it is appropriate. At this point awareness shifts and locates the seer's attention, in its corresponding intent, upon the circumstances at hand.

Q: Is it appropriate to say that the pre-ordained force can be understood as the intent of eternity? And if so, is the seer's responsibility and impeccability then to inquire of their heart about what the imagery is informing them of and acquiesce to the dictates of eternity appropriately?

In other words, is the heart and third eye's connective function a guiding beacon for the seer with respect to complex situations as mentioned earlier, whereas the third eye's function when disconnected from a pure heart can plunge the seer into confusion?

A: As I have stated before, a seer can be consumed by drama in the initial stages. When one begins to see, the heart knows immediately what it has received. If one doesn't intuitively resonate with understanding then one must wait patiently for the inevitability of the circumstance to unfold. The third eye conveys this seeing in combination with the heart's essence.

Everything seen is automatically known. There is nothing to be questioned, only events to be observed. One's impeccability will determine whether or not their integrity will be actively applied to the circumstance at hand.

Q: I have heard before of something known as *the third attention* being described very vaguely as an abstract state existing only beyond the point of physical death, or at the end of one's journey on this planet. To what extent, if any, does the abstraction and finality of this idea overlap with what you have described as the outcome of this book upon the perceiver?

A: The outcome of the techniques and the information in this book deliver the warrior to a state where they take nothing for granted. Even though we are timeless, we are not immortal.

Q: Other authors speak of people having two, three or four *prongs*. You speak of having two, three or four hundred energy compartments. Are the *prongs* made up of one hundred energy compartments as you describe?

A: The luminous field of every human being has a particular pressure. One can perceive this pressure by merely standing next to somebody. It is not too dissimilar to sitting a basketball and a medicine ball next to each other. They are the same circumference yet you know through your own personal experience that the basketball is vacuous and the medicine ball is dense.

Someone who has two prongs (or two large energy compartments, which correlates to two hundred third eye dreaming cells) has less pressure. This pressure aligns with their predetermined destiny. The corresponding net then is flung as far as the internal pressure permits. As I have said before, this does not diminish the capacity of any individual, regardless of status.

Each capacity necessitates the energetic correspondence that is obviously needed in our reality. Once again I will use the description of the medicine ball and the basketball. Once they are thrown into water one sinks to the depths while the other floats upon the surface. Each are thresholds and without these corresponding elements there would be no fluctuations in the universe at large.

To answer your question succinctly, the phenomenon of each corresponding compartment can be perceived. It is felt as a pressure and has been given the name *compartment*, to identify it from a syntactical vantage point. Yet this image does not entirely portray the full impact of seeing.

True seeing is what a warrior witnesses on their journey. Even though we each receive from our own energetic perspectives, as is being made apparently obvious here, I will say, do not perceive a limitation. We are all meant to be what is meant to be for all of us.

Here I will speak to those of you who have two hundred compartments. Be reassured that the journey of a nagual sustains and fortifies through that gravity the energy fields that are light. You are not limited. You are only limited when the very structure of our reality is being interfered with; thus the true journeys that can be made are thwarted within this reality.

As we traverse within our companionship with each other we comprehensively move into the unknown, whether we realize it or not.

This is an experience that I have contained within my memory. I returned from a task. I was luminous, spherical in shape. I was accompanied by some human companions who have two hundred compartments.

As we returned from the unknown we first appeared as units, as energetic information, luminous balls. Before that, our field had been compressed so extensively by the unknown that we looked like distant stars fading in the darkness. As we returned to those who could not venture into the depths they nestled close to us.

The energy that exuded from myself and my companions vibrated with the unusual frequency of where we had been and as we integrated the ones who waited for us absorbed the information. Through this osmosis their energetic field became denser, thereby allowing them to shift from one crucial threshold to another in correspondence to the frequency delivered.

In turn, those who receive will transmit to those who inquire in the energetic luminous field, which is the veiled reality that our third eye capacity can see.

Q: "The techniques in this book will invariably change this fixation, so that mankind can step delicately into what is known as *the third attention*: a slipstream of magic that is invariably guided by the dictums of eternity. On this tenuous thread the way of the modern seer is now being revealed, yet these revelations have only transmitted what was already known."

"Thus a teacher is a conduit, giving the tools of independence to those who seek what they have forgotten, a reminder of the energetic medium that gives substance to the gateless way, which is found through acknowledgement of that which previously could not be seen."

I heard you mention once that the techniques you give in this book are useful to a point, and once the warrior crosses the threshold that the method must be let go of. I also remember you giving a gentle warning about the tendencies of those involved in various sects and groups, pursuing the same liberation that we seek, to cling to practices beyond their usefulness.

Can you elaborate more on this? How will we know that it is time to let go? What is it about the tendency towards obsessive ritualization that is so dangerous?

Also, you mention that the techniques given to you are unique with respect to what is being taught elsewhere in terms of energetic movements and practices. How can we defend against the tendency to cultivate a separatist attitude of *us versus them* in terms of having certain information that other sects do not have?

It seems so prevalent, this divisive tendency... *We've got the right way, the right view, and you do not.* I see it everywhere... Christian denominations... Buddhist divisions and sects... martial arts disciplines... nations... races... genders. The list goes on and on.

How can we uphold the integrity and purity of the practice without watering it down, while at the same time cultivating an attitude of union and love and cooperation with our fellow seekers of freedom?

A: The techniques that I am teaching and have taught in terms of the gazing in this book have their usefulness, and when this phase is at an end the eyes will open and *see* what has been prompted through the gazing, which will naturally continue to unfold. Once this occurs then new horizons are automatically pursued.

It is when someone learns methods from a teacher who does not allow them to be free - via the fact that the teacher does not see - that these sects have their life path governed by intellectuality and the control that surrounds the delineations within that particular frame of reference.

Fortunately, as we head towards the year 2012 and beyond,

those who reach a threshold will see where they have been captured, thereby determining their own freedom. Here is where a teacher celebrates that liberation, their very independence, even knowing that their path may be fraught with trials and tribulations from that point onwards.

Our tendency as human beings to deny one another our rightful place in the world is definitely rife at the moment. If someone were to go and learn a movement that was pleasing to their eye and made their body feel happy then this is where they need to be.

If someone were to come to learn from me and if what they previously learned becomes obsolete then they will practice the physical movements that I have obtained from my benefactor. If need be, people are quite willing and able to walk away and live their life in whichever discipline they choose. This should be the way.

I will answer one question here that you haven't asked about the movements and the ritualization of movements, and why it is important for the body to be immersed in routine. It is because the body likes it.

If a person learns something and their body likes it they will practice it and this will have an effect on their cardiovascular system, enhancing their capacity to eliminate toxins and clear the electrical pathways within the body. This person will be healthier and live a longer and happier life.

As for what I teach, the same principle applies. I transit *Dragon's Tears* to introduce the initiate to the blue spectrum of light, which is also what is taught in this book in terms of plant gazing. Remember, most plants emanate the blue spectrum of electromagnetism.

I also teach *Awakening the Energy Body* and various other disciplines that take around three to four hours to accomplish if done all at once. It is not necessary for everybody to do everything that I do.

Everybody chooses their own thresholds. Until an individual wants to break those thresholds they can move to wherever they please within the system I have, or another system of their pleasing. The fact is that the body needs movement to stay young, healthy and clear.

Some practices have greater potential, in terms of opening chakras and allowing the body to absorb various types of electromagnetic energy. The body knows when this happens, without a doubt.

What I have just conveyed, to answer your next question about political and social groups, religions and sects, is that it is vitally important to allow the wind to blow the pollen from a flower. It will land where it will. That very same pollen will be carried from one flower to another, cultivating and harvesting and strengthening through the availability presenting itself. It is within mankind's desire to control another's true destiny that the trouble is embedded.

When we learn to see collectively, we will know where to give and when to receive. Our choices will be governed by the heart and this will be communally supported. Otherwise as a species we are finished.

In equal measure, those that have more must love those that have less, and those who have less will love those that have given more of themselves to equal the playing field, with a gesture of kindness that has both hands turned up and never one hidden behind the back. As our heart beats, so then will our steps be recognized.

Q: How do you engage in routines of physical practice and simultaneously remain free from the compromising attributes of ritualization? Discipline can limit us.

A: By practicing without attaching yourself to any form of outcome other than good health and happiness.

Q: What determines the difference?

A: The characteristics of the practitioner.

Q: When you refer to a woman potentially going into a deeper state of morbidity, are you referring to a kind of fatigue that represents hypersensitivity?

I see this a lot, as an imbalanced aspect of *sensitivity*, when the womb and third eye are sensitive to information yet are not yet in a stabilized field, and it relates to the channel connecting womb, heart and third eye - known as the Sea of Blood. If this is the state you refer to, do you have any knowledge also about the function of the blood and the womb in relation to a seer seeing?

A: The imbalance comes about from morbidity due to the fact that the influx of information is overwhelming; not for the seer, but as a result of the woman becoming impatient with behavior that may be seen as imbecilic, for their speed is tremendous in comparison to those they wish to impart the transmission to.

Obviously blood and chi are major components within the essence of male and female. All is determined by the ensuing force that momentarily occasions the awareness that is open to it at the point of reception.

Q: Do you have any advice for a woman, or man, who has fallen into this deeper state of morbidity? Am I correct in understanding that this can come about through overwhelm of perceptual influx for a developing seer, who has not yet learned to handle themselves through controlled folly? Or perhaps in a naturally psychically gifted person who does not realize themselves?

I feel this is a very different learning curve for those whose third eye develops through practices, compared to those who seem to just have it switched on. In the latter group, learning arts such as *controlled folly* is often hit and miss, until they find supporting information and teachings, such as in this book. Is there any energetic or technique based advice to apply for those in a state of such morbidity?

A: Just relax and let the flow of events unfold in front of you without interfering. The controlling factor that a seer may experience here has to do with needing to learn to detach themselves from the fact that they want to control the outcome. Even though they feel propelled to intervene, more often than not they should not interfere with the natural course of events.

If the circumstances really do require intervention, obviously this is different and action should be taken. As you progress on your life path your truth will be applied and spoken appropriately in comparison to your personal power.

Q: "A seer will only speak of what is seen, not what is known"

Can you elaborate about the transmissions that occur when seeing is contained in impeccability?

A: The knowing of a seer, when spoken, breaks the original boundaries of what is known intellectually. I have often said that to be in a state of acquiescence is the key. This means to be in a state of levity.

When one ascends, they gather pertinent information in correspondence to the circumstances. As the humbleness of a warrior precedes them, they choose to wait for words to erupt from the heart center that are not circumnavigated by the need for validation.

Nevertheless, this does not mean that a warrior shrinks from their responsibility: they know if eternity necessitates the knowing. In the limbs of a human being much information can be stored, bodily information.

When the pressures of eternity have delivered blow after blow to the seer's personal world, the body becomes attuned and receptive and does not keep as a script what has already been seen but knows definitely if they see something similar or the same again via the fact that the body becomes alerted. And there they wait, watching gently that which unfolds.

Also it is important to establish an understanding around the word impeccability. It means to be without sin, and to be without sin is to be without regret. There are no regrets if one applies themselves impeccably to their circumstances.

There is one very interesting factor here that I have not explained. By virtue of the third eye being activated, even if one is unaware, every person you come in contact with - to the smallest eye gesture, to a passing hello, even loving someone from afar - has far-reaching effects. More than you would expect.

By virtue of the fact that you read this, I am obligated to contact you, even though we haven't met. I will come and see you through the projection of my third eye capacity. And as I see you, you see me, even if you don't remember, and each of us sees each other right up to the moment of our death. Every minute amount of information that has been and will be is communicated via the broad expansive touch of the third eye.

So in essence you have seen my trials and tribulations as I have seen yours. You have seen my death as I have witnessed yours, yet we age and progress upon our path until the culmination of our inevitability touches ever so gently the fragility of our human form to expand beyond its known parameters.

We have all seen what is possible to have been seen and what will be known. We are all capable and powerful beyond measure.

Two weeks after a very well known celebrity died, his presence swept through my being. And he knew, as I knew, that I saw and he saw a combined effect that was the interlinking, not only between he and myself, but between all of humanity.

So as you can see, our responsibility is more than immense. It is absolutely all-encompassing, and the way to harmoniously proceed with eternity is to endeavor to humbly give ourselves in service to that which presents itself.

Q: When you refer to not possessing internal imagery, do you mean possessing is responding with a kind of language and behavior that is egoic? E.g. presented with confidence, claiming to know fully what this vision is, yet through this behavior simultaneously seeking validation and recognition for having vision.

A: To have something internally sustained as a visual image, speaks of containment. This is the first stage and yes, many people claim and possess these visions. The trick is to make no claim and set them free, so that one's state of being is in full reception of that which can't be spoken nor seen yet is conveyed externally as an image that speaks to the seer; instead of the seeker speaking of their vision.

Q: When seeing becomes external and is accompanied with knowing of itself in detail, how is this related to pure knowing arriving without a visual component? Is this also considered to be the same form of *seeing*?

A: Seeing can be delivered without imagery. Knowing can be known without this component and when you have arrived at this state you will speak the hearts of others and know the minds of men from a distance.

Q: Loosening up the fixated view brings a well of happenings and *seeing*s, experiencing all that was and is as if new - never seen before as such - things that escape notice when in a state of sleep.

If seeing is not visual by definition, can it be felt? Physically maybe, as a pressure, not only in the area that feels as your 'extended head' but in the throat and stomach especially. Can this be seeing? Opening the third eye?

Or is it the influence of something manipulating you, a shadow, another person, 'un'-emptiness or attachments in yourself that you now feel? Or are they actually one and the same? I'm not always 'certain, without a doubt' about these things, so I'm not sure about the ways it may manifest itself either.

A: Here you are basically asking about the dark arts and the effect that they can have upon a seer. There is your normal common Joe that has ill intentions and bad thoughts. They are felt as a pressure in the solar plexus and, depending on how stifling that person's energy is, the throat is affected.

As I said previously, the seeing of a warrior becomes

absorbed in the body and then begins to recognize various influences through the frequencies experienced, transmitted telepathically. This has to do with the third eye capacity of knowing as a result of the residual effect of being subject to humanity at large.

There is an old saying: *Dumb is dangerous.* This refers to people who do not realize the full implications of their doings upon another's life path. In a lot of circumstances outcomes can be devastating if the negativity is relentless in its repetitiveness.

Unfortunately many people take delight in inflicting upon others, due to the fact that they can't free themselves and need another to be ensnared so that they cannot escape into a higher or happier frequency.

The heart and the third eye have upper and lower containment fields. The lower containment field is the region where the manifest world in all of its diversity relates directly. The upper portions of the third eye and heart seek freedom and levity and bask in the full light of the happiness that sustains oneself.

A person practicing black magic will do many things, tirelessly, to sever the connection of the person they wish to influence to their upper compartments. They can do this by disrupting sleep, by poisoning, by gossiping, through incantations, or in any number of ways, especially if they have obtained an item that belongs to the one they wish to inflict their vengeance upon.

Blood is one of the most sought after items for people who practice this art, so it is vitally important to keep your private belongings; your hair, your blood, your nails, any bodily secretions and photographs, out of reach of a black magician, especially when traveling in undeveloped countries.

The effect of this art, as I have said, creates a pressure on the chakra system in correspondence to the intention outlaid. When one is under psychic attack it is usually more pronounced on the two days of the first appearance of the crescent moon. This is the time that the moon is just visible and all else is out of sight.

All phases of the moon till the full moon can be dangerous as intentions cast from the time of the crescent moon till the full moon have magnified consequences. The collective gravity of people practicing black magic (and those caught in a level of consciousness that is not beneficial for others or themselves) using these times to enhance the impact of their designs has a concentrating effect.

Nevertheless, be strong. It is all here to test us. Even if someone achieves taking away your happiness, plan to move away so you can sustain an environment that emanates the natural joyousness of the heart's freedom.

Q: "In order to expand individually and collectively, communal conductivity is where we need to direct our awareness. This conductivity demands that each knows what has already been universally organized and submits to what is presented and does not dictate through individual desire - yet individual desire governs the dictums of awareness for the bidding becomes the true expression of one's individuality."

"They interact by virtue of our wants and desires and this becomes our capacity to influence the structure of reality through the effect of the incalculable force of our third eye capacity to expand beyond our wildest expectations via the fact that it is eternally connected to an unknown factor, which conversely is also influenced by our socially determined limitations."

How do we transform desire from being one of the primary mechanisms that keeps us trapped into that which facilitates the pure expression of our capacity to co-create?

A: By being a witness to our circumstances and only acting appropriately. This integrity becomes the warrior's response. It is personal, yet impersonal.

Q: What is the blue spectrum and why is it important to become aware of it?

A: The blue spectrum is the highest frequency of light. It is what one develops when they practice *Dragon's Tears* and what they see when they do the gazing. It opens and activates the third eye in correspondence with the crown, allowing the heart to facilitate the dictums of eternity through the throat chakra.

Q: Often information just arrives, without a conscious inquiry. Sometimes we inquire with varying degrees of consciousness that we are asking, even through simply having curiosity. Is there a difference in the kind of information that arrives with no inquiry?

The reason I ask is because, once we begin to consciously seek, we can easily end up stalking information, or answers. I have often found that the information that arrives when there is no direct question is more expansive or complete somehow. Is that due to the level of emptiness of the inquirer, which depicts the nature of inquiry and response?

A: Yes, the emptiness of the inquirer will determine what is seen.

Q: I have read descriptions of naguals as being energetically asymmetric. If this is true, what is the energetic function of this asymmetry?

A: Anything that has this configuration in the luminous field would cause disparities that are not negative if the one who possesses it has discipline. Very similar to throwing a ball that has another quarter of a ball fused to it. It will spin and make complex patterns.

In some cases this causes enormous amounts of growth for others, by virtue of the fact that the awareness distorts the field of perception; and to take into consideration that distortion one must have enormous prowess to assimilate the extra influx. Others may utilize the information obtained to expand upon original boundaries.

The only drawback is that from a symmetrical viewpoint, the expanded context will be reallocated into others' awareness as reason, and then they will reformulate the insights to suit the capacities of their own consciousness, adapted in terms of their agenda. This very reasonableness, strangely enough, distorts the original information away from its abstract meaning. Thus dogma occurs in defense of one thing in comparison to another.

There have been many teachers who have used hallucinogens to create awareness in pockets of attention that are not being utilized, causing the same effect. When the energy bubble returns to its original shape it causes a thinning of the field. Thus the danger in these instances is an influx or an outpouring. In either case, imbalance occurs.

Q: " When one sees the internal pictorial imagery of another there is never confusion. The third eye is precise in its seeing. What can become confusing is that if this first type of seeing, which is internal, is then coupled with the harbored emotionality of the individual that has become aware, then doubt may arise from unresolved feelings that interfere with the seeing itself."

"What I am saying here is that all of the imagery that is internal, we must allow to externalize itself and not possess the images that appear inwardly, for they do not belong to us. They belong to the final command of our inevitability, our death."

There is a particular type of experience I've had, especially recognizable after practicing the gazing techniques in this book, that relates to the internal vs. external imagery.

I was riding back home in a taxi and all of a sudden I had a video running in my head about a scandal tape from a few years back. I hadn't seen this tape and so I couldn't have known what it looked like, yet it was now running in my mind as internal visual content.

I realized that the imagery belonged to the taxi driver, as I didn't have any emotionality attached to what I was now viewing and there was no reason why I should now be seeing it. After reading about letting this imagery become external, I am wondering whether this is the type of internal seeing that could in time become outwardly witnessed?

A: When a seer perceives external imagery it is usually in correspondence with the influx of eternity as insight, which pertains to the growth of the two individuals or many.

As for the internal imagery you have described, this is a valid insight in terms of the perspective you have evolved in order to become aware of this. The experience you have had is clear in terms of the threshold that you have arrived upon.

When a seer maps the unknown, quite often the realizations are without imagery or they are external. If a seer was to sit in a taxi as you did, they would know through their seeing that the image portrayed internally is belonging to the person that they are traveling with.

A warrior may be in the very same circumstance and hear a voice inside their head. Knowing it is not theirs, they listen and know it belongs to another. This is in most cases only a script that necessitates what needs to be realized.

The third eye accommodates feeling, hearing, and seeing. Each circumstance will be governed by your reception, alerting you to the attention focused.

Q: After one begins to experience the internal imagery and auditory phenomena of other beings, you say that the next step is to experience the images externally. Is there another threshold beyond this?

A: Yes there is. As the warrior progresses upon their path, the internal imagery and auditory phenomena that become externalized are a momentary point of reference that educate the body, in terms of informing it of what is occurring beyond the linear process. The next phase is that the body of the warrior becomes absorbed in that reception, continually bombarded by what can only be described as the unknown factor.

When a seer reaches this perspective, which has no frame of reference and cannot be speculated about, there is a form of unification that one becomes aware of through their body consciousness.

I can only describe it as a form of resignation that knows all the possibilities in terms of their arrangements; yet the seer stands back and allows everything to unfold in every which way, knowing that what is being witnessed is a pre-determined event that cannot be struggled against.

This is where a warrior becomes absolutely aware of the fact that they must embrace adversity, as their body challenges the very fundamental rudimentary roots of the construct that presents itself.

Here a seer discovers their greatest adversary, a deep dark influence beyond the cognition of those who are being driven by it, yet who are convinced that the way they are proceeding is correct.

Unbeknownst to them, behind their eyes, there are beings

that seek to infiltrate our very world, our living construct; thereby channeling reality, sustaining a lower conceptualization and thus disabling our capacity to evolve as a humanity.

Q: In the early stages of developing the ability to see and know through our third eye capacity and our intuitive insight, how do we navigate the trap of becoming too 'certain', and therefore potentially rigid and limited within our perspective?

A: At this stage of developing third eye function, a particular type of clarity erupts. One can become so clear that they are right, yet there are so many factors to be taken into consideration that the subtleties will inevitably deliver you to another perception, which means you must remain in a state of impassive abeyance; of waiting for what is to come. Then you realize that maybe you weren't right.

There is a certain stage of clarity where self-righteousness in terms of stalking the social perspective blinds the warrior, due to the fact that they have been offended by what they have become aware of.

This revolves back to their inherent socially conditioned nature; to feel important enough to intervene on behalf of someone else's life, where they truly can't see the depth of complexity of the life of the one they are interfering with.

One interesting aspect of this is that the intervention of this stage of warriorship allows a more powerful seer to stand back and observe the folly as it progresses, which in actual fact is the natural course of events that was meant to occur.

It is not so much the words and actions of others but what emanates from their body that presses upon us, demanding conformity and alignment. Talking itself is often repetitive and meaningless compared to the cellular communications we receive, on the level of our body consciousness.

We are re-educating the body consciousness to become aware that it knows what is going on. The intellect has become so dominant that the body consciousness is dwarfed, thus blocking access to insight.

Q: Can you elaborate on what you mean by not dreaming?

Do you refer to becoming lucid in dreaming; *awakening* within dreaming so that one may then dream in the void, as you did with the guidance of your benefactors? Do you refer to dissolving all dreaming, even those dreams that are lucid in which we may be receiving teachings, or such?

Some see it that we are always dreaming, even if we dream of no dream, so to speak. What does this experience of not-dreaming look like during sleep? Or do you mean that the technique and process of commanding yourself not to dream creates a new stage of becoming aware?

A: Commanding yourself not to dream allows for a new state of becoming aware by virtue of the fact that all the excessive energy put into the imagery to sustain a dream is then re-routed back into the power of the third eye to see – either internally or externally - or to know without the influx of visual imagery by obtaining the basic vibratory core of what arrives through feeling. But this is not a feeling in terms of experiencing *emotion*.

It is the awakening of body consciousness to assimilate the influx of information as it arrives. Here the body thinks and not the mind. Even though the body does not have a process of thinking, it knows itself at the point of arrival.

My initiation into the realm of the nagual was transmitted to my body consciousness by advanced light beings. In my case I learnt from a man who lived in the 17th century, the old nagual Lujan. He was in cahoots with the nagual Juan Matus and another, known as the Tenant, who imparted the most profound wisdom of his living experiences to the naguals he touched throughout generations.

The Tenant is the man I came to know as Malaiyan, a most gentle and poetic warrior. The influx of information that pertained to my life path arrived in the 20th century.

Through the course of events of my life and the life of my benefactor, his third eye capacity traversed the known limits of his universe, which became the comprehensible limits of my own consciousness, in terms of my capacity to assimilate a third eye perspective that knows no limitation. When you truly look at it clearly, we are one. There is no limit to our abilities as human beings.

To have an ethereal intervention, as took place in my case, clearly illustrates the power that all my benefactors had obtained throughout their lifetimes. This power itself transmits the possibility, or better yet, the *reality*, of our capacity to interact dimensionally.

To come to terms with a non-linear perspective is to stand back and observe that which is our predetermined destiny. In other words, to accept what we can't change.

SEEKING ALIGNMENT

Now I would like to introduce you to non-sequential time continuums. Bear in mind these two extracts are sequentially out of alignment. Here you meet my words as they are now in this paragraph and in the next account you see my words as they were. This is an exercise in precognition.

You will read what *was* yet remember what *is* in this chapter, prompting the elasticity of your innate precognitive ability to reactivate itself so as to circumnavigate the mind's need to validate its steps from its limited linear perspective.

A portion of my awareness was taken at age seven by my

benefactor, the old nagual Lujan, which initiated my third eye awakening. This experience directly relates to alternate realities that appear as dreams, yet are as solid as the world we walk in.

Due to these events the other aspects of my totality, which remained here in the physical world, were unable to apply their attention in a strictly linear sense, as takes place in the chambers of formal education.

Later in life, the part of me that was taken as a child was returned to me and I then became the awakened man, able to transmit to others linear concepts originating from a multilateral perspective.

What this means is that the pressure applied to me through another's attention releases the information embedded within my consciousness that otherwise would not arise, as I am not operating from my mind and in fact prefer to remain without thoughts.

I have documented my experiences thoroughly in my first book, *The Art of Stalking Parallel Perception*. To provide new readers with a deeper understanding of the encounters that lead me to the multi-lateral perspective from which I operate, the following two excerpts have been taken from this book.

The Dream Walker

On one moonlit night, I opened the gate to our front yard, not to leave but to return. I had been gone for a while and had forgotten where I had been as I proceeded down the front path that was lined with daisies.

Even though the flowers were stationary, they seemed to reach out and press forward and in that gentle gesture caress my being. They were waiting for me; they knew I was there. Each one was aware and they conveyed themselves wordlessly, their beauty so utterly profound.

I approached the house and as I walked onto the balcony, the doorway appeared to devour me within its shadow. When I turned back towards the path the moonlight acknowledged that I had gone, but was still mocking me within its subtleties. It was the twinkle in my eye.

I turned to look down the length of the balcony and saw moonbeams streaming through the windows. The light was soft and sensual and filled my being with a sense of awe and beauty. I ventured along those well-worn boards and the sound of my feet reverberated, softly echoing my presence upon the wooden floor.

As I passed each bedroom window I was lost to myself, and had forgotten who was behind those frames. I turned the corner and approached the side entrance, where I looked through the glass and then entered gently. Immediately to my left the doorway leading to my mother's room was half ajar.

I pushed it open and walked in. There I stood by her bed, watching her sleeping. I was unaware of how long I was gazing, totally absorbed within a realization that she did not sleep like me. She slept like something else.

Suddenly, my mother opened her eyes and lunged forward.

Screeching, she grabbed me by the shoulders. "What are you doing, watching me in my bed?" she seethed, and her clenched teeth made her look like a ferocious animal.

She shook me violently till I awoke, but awake like her, not aware like I was. I trembled and my teeth chattered for hours as I realized that I had been ambushed, and that her reality was so much harsher than the one that I was previously immersed within.

What I need to mention now is what I saw in my mother's eyes when she lunged at me. Despite the fact that I was sleepwalking, my memory of what I witnessed is acute and has haunted me to this very day.

The beast that is described in biblical texts, and the shadow awareness that has been referred to throughout this book, is what leapt at me through my mother's arms and viewed me from behind her eyes, before she became aware of what she was doing.

When I was watching her within that dream walking state, I was seeing within dimensions. What I saw was a being, whispering and talking coercively, directing her dream attention, unbeknownst to her.

When this Luciferian presence noticed that I could see it, it lunged towards me through her body in an attempt to destabilize that window view that I had accessed. From that time the onslaughts of these entities have never ceased. Their pursuit of me has been relentless since then, for I saw at that time something that I shouldn't have been able to.

What I am to explain now is very difficult to understand. When I access this memory, and realize the implications of that recollection, the energy that exudes from my heart center becomes explosive.

When that beast reached through my mother's arms and grabbed me so that I would be caught within a complex web, a man intervened. There I was, a shocked seven-year old boy with my eyes wide open and my mother grasping my arms fiercely, glaring at me as if murder was her next intention.

Simultaneously, I was in total darkness, standing in a void that seemed to want to consume me, with a venomous and possessive shadow racing towards me at a terrifying velocity and the full intention of stealing my soul, or my awareness, from that point on.

I was paralyzed with fear. But before this disturbing entity reached my childhood form within dreams, that man suddenly appeared, standing between the shadow and myself. He was dressed in oriental black leather armor. He lifted his left hand to the height of his shoulder as if to say 'Stop', yet not a word was spoken.

There was a ripple in that universe, something tangible and so powerful. It was my benefactor. He turned around and picked me up within his arms, and what manifested around us was his realm. Once we were completely surrounded by the velvety darkness of the void, he gently put me down.

"Now we will wait for you to find yourself," he whispered, and slowly retreated into an obscure hallway.

Empathic Dreaming

I am the dreamer who dreamt my child, who was taught by the dream maker, the old Nagual* Lujan. He taught my child and my child returned to me, the dreamer, who became the awakened man who transmits the inner child through the stories of the dreams. The old Nagual Lujan, also known as Master Lo Ban**, is my benefactor. He found me in the dream of an adult.

I was in a building, in an elevator on the eightieth floor, when a visceral fear suddenly engulfed me. I knew that it was going to plummet to the ground and all at once I was travelling

---

* The Nagual is a leader and the bearer of altered perceptions.
** Lo Ban literally translates to: *Elegantly flourishing spirals*.

downward at a massive speed. I bent my knees and grabbed hold of the railing, afraid that my legs would be snapped backwards from the impact. As I braced myself, I heard an explosion, and then a thunderous sound manifested all around me. I had arrived and was not injured at all.

There were dust particles in the air as I tentatively walked out of the elevator into semi-darkness. I couldn't define the walls or the size of the room, and as I was scanning the environment a feeling of great oppression hit my chest. This sensation transformed into the growl of a jaguar that was lurking in the shadows. I heard that animal from different positions all at once, as if I was surrounded. And I was.

Fear once again engulfed me. I did not want to be mauled and die that way. Grappling with my mounting apprehension, I looked upwards and turned that intensity into the growl itself. The whole scene was surreal, unbelievable to me, as though I was watching myself in a movie and in the same instant hearing myself ferociously roaring like a wild cat cornered.

At that moment, I noticed envelopes falling from above. As

they hit the ground, I realized there were men in the room hiding in the darkness, which frightened me in a way that I was not really familiar with.

They were watching me. I felt their intentions piercing through the fabric that was my being. At that point I knew they were testing me. I lent down to pick up one of the envelopes from the floor and saw a name. "What the…? Why would I need this?" I asked myself.

The room suddenly turned black, and what appeared in front of me was a long rectangular corridor. As I became accustomed to the atmosphere that was confronting my body on a very deep level, it began to expand, allowing me to see more clearly what was there. I looked into it and realized that I would have to take one step up, yet I dared not, for I knew the energetic implication of walking upon that new threshold was beyond my strength at that moment.

Peering into the obscurity, I saw a figure standing at the end of that ominous chamber. He looked like an oriental warrior, clad in ancient, traditional black leather armor. He stepped forward, and when his right foot hit what seemed to be a stone floor, the atmosphere rippled as if it had tangible substance. He then left the ground and flew toward me horizontally through the air.

Upon his approach, the pressure that ensued from his body entered me, and every fiber of my being became infused with his presence. He landed in a half-kneeling stance with his right knee to the floor, and his left foot firmly planted in front of him. His right forearm shielded his downward gaze, and his left palm pushed toward the ground by his side.

The name *Lujan** entered my body, whilst a golden sphere with a blue glow was simultaneously propelled toward me from the center of his being and stabilized itself within my heart.

"This is yours to give to the dreamer, little one."

When he spoke, I realized that I was a child and upon that moment the dream scene disappeared.

The old oriental warrior Lujan, my benefactor, instructed

---

* Lujan (pronounced Lu-han): to be luminous

the small boy who was in front of him to wait for himself to arrive. Yet upon the point that I appeared I was a man of the age of forty. The moment I saw the ancient sage directly in front of me, the frame that was my adult being disintegrated and all that was left was a seven-year-old child.

I had found myself. Upon the emergence of that finding, I had been transported to a sequence of time where my adult form did not exist, yet I was forty years old. This does not make sequential sense I know. It can only be experienced.

As you proceed and walk with me deep within these pages you will begin to realize an altering of your body consciousness will occur. There is one more excerpt that I will insert here, and it is an account of when I was split three ways by the old nagual, my benefactor. However, it will not be in the way that you will expect, that will give you the capacity to understand what has happened to me.

Once you begin to see you will know irrefutably that what has been written holds within it secrets that are brought to light, yet the unveiling will not be something that one can become conscious of purposely.

When a human being is taught, especially when that human being is a nagual, they are shown that they have a capacity to move multi-dimensionally; in and around the frameworks of time - forward and backwards - and yet operate linearly.

The sense of your own belief and programming must be overcome to even comprehend one's natural ability to interact in a world that has dimensionality within its sight.

Our eyes walk upon worlds expressed within words that collide with the capacity to know and see in comparison to the matrix that you possess as a conscious being. This is the third eye capacity to conceive of and to feel what you cannot feel; to see what you perceive you cannot see and to listen to what is inaudible.

When the old nagual appeared within that hallway, and simultaneously intervened in front of me within dimension when I was a child, he was splitting my attention within the fabric of the universal eye.

SEEKING ALIGNMENT

One facet would live in this realm - our living construct - as a seven year old child and progress within this worldly dimension. Another would wait with him patiently, while the third was taken and shown worlds beyond worlds and transmissions of movement and knowledge that are now being disclosed. This occurred for thirty three years and as you emerge, so do I.

We are all intertwined. My heart is your heart. Your heart is mine and the net of man is interconnected dimensionally. Thus our futures together emerge into a new era.

I have not known of, nor yet heard of, anybody experiencing this type of intimate dimensional communion: to have a master formulate a world in front of you that is seemingly of your own making, combining present, future and past into a visual matrix that leads one to understand what they were never meant to see.

Fortunately my destiny is as such and here you walk upon my words and see the actions of a man, my benefactor, that to this day I recall, yet the very thing I perceive escapes me. In essence these are the workings of the universal third eye applying itself within dimension.

I have also been very fortunate to be under the tutelage of don Juan Matus; not as a teacher within the living construct but as a benefactor beyond the grasp of daily reality. At the crucial juncture where he came into my life he used the name Zakai.

All that you see and uncover through my writing was not only transmitted in words. My benefactor's very gestures held within them energetic units of information that became the transmissions that are the culmination of all that you find through my discoveries.

We can be in gratitude, I realize, for their labors; their unyielding intent to go beyond the known reaches of the tangible universe and bring back the essential petals of the eternally flowering lotus of knowledge.

Upon the recounting of the *Dream Walker,* I was deeply affected. I knew there was something trapped within me that wanted to surface in my perception that I could not comprehend. I felt a little bit stuck and went to bed that evening with a feeling of despondency over my inability to fathom what I needed to know for my own life.

"Awake with you."

I heard Zakai's familiar voice beckoning my awareness to join him.

"Come with me now my friend and sit by the void. Look within the depths of that which is in front of you. I believe that we all should be told what is necessary. I would like now to share with you a story of power and this story is yours."

"Unknown to you, you have been affected quite profoundly by the old nagual. It would take you a lifetime to recover and explain to yourself what I am to explain to you now. The reason I am giving this information to you at this point is to avert any confusion on your part on what took place between you and the old nagual thirty-three years ago."

"When I called you tonight you were preoccupied. When I focused on your being I knew immediately what was occurring. The feeling that flooded my luminosity when I focused on you was the same feeling I experienced when I saw the old nagual split one of your dream compartments, which belong to the honeycomb maze of awareness, into two. Before I explain any further I will tell you where the old nagual gained the knowledge to accomplish such a monumental feat."

"Centuries ago the old nagual was introduced to an extremely old shaman and had become so intimately connected with him that he taught him secrets. One of these secrets has been utilized through our contact with you."

"Look now deep within the void and recall that vision of the honeycomb compartments that I once directed you to view within that expansiveness. While you gaze deep into this vision that lies in front of you I will prompt you to remember your own compartments."

As Zakai said this the honeycomb compartments of awareness appeared within the void, but this time I was not viewing another's configuration, I was viewing my own. I began to feel elated to think that I could see myself within such complexity yet still be sitting by the void, physically intact.

Zakai interrupted me and said, "Now focus and I will give

you the story that is yours, then you will be released from your feelings of anguish because of the fact that you cannot recall that which is so embedded. I do this for you because recovering these units of information would be otherwise impossible to access until your journey was completed. As I said, it is better to know and understand so that one can survey that which seems inconceivable."

"As you look, silence will enter deep within you. What you will see now is one of those techniques that this old shaman taught the old nagual and this was a gift to him, among the many that he was given."

As I looked into the void I once again saw the nagual clad in black oriental leather armor, standing between me and that shadow that I had described in my recounting, which had left me in a state of deep and profound contemplation. I saw him pick that child up in his arms and then I saw something beyond belief.

When he had laid me down in that vastness he performed some strange movements, casting threads of light that left visual impressions of infinity symbols, figure eights that dropped gently into the compartment that was being cast upon. Somehow these gestures unfolded me into that honeycomb maze that I was watching with Zakai within the void.

I then saw the nagual take one of these compartments and separate it from the collective. When this was done he reassembled my being by clapping his hands in a way that is incomprehensible to me even to this day. That part of me that became reorganized returned to me in the living construct where I lay shaking in my mother's arms after being awoken from my sleepwalking journey.

(Bear in mind now that I am seeing these images in front of me in multiples and for you to understand what I am explaining now you must attempt a multi-lateral assimilation to conceive of what I am to outline.)

Zakai then said to me, "Break now your fixation from that portion of awareness that shows you the child that has been awoken within the living construct. Go with your awareness to that compartment that the Dream Maker holds. See the magic that is to occur in front of you."

SEEKING ALIGNMENT

I gazed into the void and saw the nagual with one of my dream compartments, floating within a vastness. He was once again executing a strange movement that spiraled towards his feet and simultaneously coiled upwards to the zenith. I saw once more an infinity symbol manifesting as a momentary impression, following the coiling motion of his hands in the center of the energetic cones he created.

This provoked a sensation within my midsection that made my chest feel like it was going to explode. At the point where I thought my torso was going to expand beyond my physical limits, the compartment that I was viewing divided and separated into two sections. What I saw then were two small children in the company of the old oriental warrior.

He said to one, "Now we will wait until you find yourself," and the other he took into an alternate dream scene where this child lived for thirty-three years. This child's name was Somai.

At this moment, Zakai intervened. "Calm yourself," he said. "You are very fortunate. The gift of power that the nagual has given to you is beyond your comprehension at this moment. This memory that you review is a time capsule of happening, which occurred beyond the temporal limits of your cognitive system."

"Know that when Somai merged with you, you were simply assimilating yourself and when you encountered yourself as a child in the Dream Maker's realm upon your reawakening thirty-three years later, that child became one with you as well."

I broke my fixation from the void to look at Zakai. "Is this the reason why I know and can do strange things?"

"Yes," he confirmed.

"The old nagual and Somai were occupied for thirty-three years and within that time Somai assimilated profound mysterious knowledge that was imparted to him, which you know now is part of you. Now that I have awoken you to what occurred so many years ago, your task will be to recall those lessons that the old nagual taught to you, not in an altered state, but in a state beyond any seer's wildest dreams."

Zakai gently grasped my hand. "Now that you know you will see more easily those things that were passed to you because you have seen what happened and how that happening occurred."

Softly squeezing my hand, he looked directly into my eyes and said.

"What a wonderful tale of power, what an awesome story to recall. Awake with you now."

Q: The old nagual spoke and said:

"Now we shall wait for you to find yourself."

I am curious what he meant by this. Was he speaking about the lessons you would need to learn in the social world before you ventured back to your power; your core; your vastness?

As I see it, when you were taken, and when your luminosity was returned occurred instantaneously, yet you had aged some thirty-three years. What was it that needed to be within these years for you? If the old nagual lived beyond time, the thirty-three years were inconsequential. Why didn't the transmission occur when you were first taken?

A: The transmission did happen immediately, yet the

sequence of time has its value with regard to the linear process that occurred. This is what is so difficult to explain, in terms of non-sequential time units of information coming together sequentially. There were many things that needed to take place for me personally as a human being.

By virtue of the fact that the old nagual took the specific compartment that he did, I was rendered mute in terms of having the capacity to assimilate information from a rote-learning perspective.

When the compartment was returned to me this capacity to learn what normal people assimilate still did not occur. I was bombarded with visual information from where I was taken to, which had transferred into physical units or movements that I obtained from the old nagual.

Q: Why was a portion of you waiting, simply waiting? What was the reason for this waiting? Why was that compartment removed only to wait? Why did the old nagual see fit to take this compartment?

A: Very astute question. To abide in absolute stillness, in complete silence, in a vastness that relayed everything yet in everything there was nothing. This experience taught me to wait and to be silent. It was necessary.

Q: What is it that must occur to free oneself from the influence of our programming? You said extrication of the internal dialogue won't completely nullify the program's effect. Is it complete dis-identification with the emotional dialogue that removes that influence? What would you suggest to another as to how to arrive absolutely upon their true selves?

A: All the information relayed in this book will answer your question. Nevertheless, it is the internal dialog and the emotional reflex that pertains to the social eddy that bind collectively all that is at the moment. This is what needs to be reviewed independently, until there is an advanced communal connectivity that sees the entrapment that coercively inhibits human awareness.

Q: How does the double relate to the compartments? Is the double one of our compartments? Does the double mirror the compartments, creating an extra set? Are the compartments of the double or of the physical (although they are energy)?

A: The third eye compartments are not the double. When these compartments are no longer utilized for dreaming the double then will centralize itself within one's human form, which in essence is luminous.

When this occurs the strength of the double will pull the spinning plates of the chakras closer to the physical body, thereby enhancing that strength and also the capacity of the double to sustain itself within this living construct.

To answer your question in another way, no one knows precisely where their double is located. It is veiled. This is a mystery for all and one only sees momentarily what the double sees. When you arrive in the spot where you have already been you know you have been there, yet the memory eludes you at the moment you arrive. It is a form of déjà vu that will permanently evade you. That is one of the reasons why the double is a mystery.

My students have often seen me arrive in the room before I

get there and are shocked physically when I disappear from the room and then suddenly walk in the door. What I was taught was to bring the double here and not to use its eyes for dreaming. The information that I am giving you here may seem confusing. There are no hard and fast answers nor rules to be applied to the double.

Q: This question may really belong to another section but I want to ask: What do you do now when the shadow presents to you through loved ones, as in this story with your mother? I realize that what one *does* is unique to each moment and situation. Is there a theoretical response that can guide integral behavior for these kinds of situations?

A: When something is asked it is never inappropriate. This question will stay here. First I will tell you that I have profound connections to many people. The bonds go beyond blood. Now you must remember that I am speaking only from my own experience.

It is no one's business to sever anybody's ties with anybody including family. So listen to my words carefully and endeavor not to live vicariously through them. This is how mistakes are made.

SEEKING ALIGNMENT

Live through your own experiences. Know through your own heart. Walk your own path until it is exhausted and when you see that your journey must change, then change it. Or your journey will change for you. Whichever way.

When I perceived that entity that coercively spoke to my mother, directing her attention, it was not only the entity that gave power to this situation; it was my mother as well. People live and as they do consequences arise. Unfortunately the consequences that unfolded before my eyes were only for me to see.

As I lay in my mother's arms with my teeth chattering from the shock of being awoken from sleepwalking, she held me tight, regretting her actions. She had been advised not to wake me while I was sleepwalking.

They only knew what they knew in those days, and this was very little. Indigenous communities still hold fast to the truth of realities beyond the world that we perceive in these disrupted modern times, but unfortunately these keepers of internal wisdom are being generationally decimated.

SEEKING ALIGNMENT

To answer your question for me is not personal. I see the lineage of my family as it is: futile and without purpose. I bear no ill will but I have no feelings, no camaraderie to speak of. I understand the limitations that beset their lives and that diminish their capacity to go beyond the social bindings, which is the web of their perception that they dare not deviate from so as to appear compliant and comfortable and never to be confronted.

Then there are those who I have come to know that weep tears of joy when we meet, who speak their deepest truths and reveal their most hidden secrets; who I call family. This includes my children. They leave knowing that what they were bound to no longer binds them, and here my heart never labors. It is always full, caring and abundant in the presence of these warriors.

They struggle with the very thing that my mother did, yet they know what they are contending with. That's the difference. For some it is the nagging mind. For others it is unrelenting emotions. They struggle to be free until the moment arises that allows them to reap their finest reward.

To go back to your question: How do you deal with friends

and family? When a moment arises that you see something appearing behind their eyes, belligerent and nasty, that wishes to harm and cause grief, the answer is: Stand back.

Allow yourself to see and know quietly what you are witnessing. Silently watch until the moment comes that the one you interact with realizes that maybe their input is detrimental. Even then don't seek personal validation. Stand silently and watch what presents itself at the moment you see it.

As you embrace the person in front of you with all of your heart, without even a whisper of what you know, through accepting silently you have dealt the most devastating blow to your potential captor; thereby allowing the embraced to understand that you see without the spoken word, thus empowering them to realize what they are doing and who they are through your kindness.

Q: Can the compartments be considered positions of awareness that each hold parts of understanding or being - of past, present, future - of teachings, memories? A sudden understanding never feels 'new' but like something already present that is simply found again.

Is it actually compartments interacting with each other or with other people's compartments that create a different constellation, so to speak? Or maybe more accurately, of certain compartments suddenly aligning, overlapping or communicating - even if temporarily – thus generating a different interaction of the parts individually, that brings about this non-rational understanding?

Is the deeper understanding and fluidity that we seek meant to make the compartments interact with each other and be conscious of the whole? Does 'total recall' occur when all the compartments are open to each other and aware of each other and what they exist as, as a whole?

A: Even though we are wholly and solely focusing on the third eye capacity to perceive in multiples, it is the swirling matrix that is the crown that universally spans out, launching the net of the third eye. In some cultures this has been called the thousand-petaled lotus.

SEEKING ALIGNMENT

Seeing an omen can be likened to the image of a flower. The petal represents the vision, the voice; the recognition of what was, what will be and what is becoming. The essential nature of precognition has been misunderstood.

What you must realize here is that precognition occurs on two levels. It is dependent upon where the seer is in terms of their alignment in comparison to what is coming.

If a vision appears internally the eye will see it as such. It will be contained and have certain parameters, guiding the seer to understand its limitations. When it is an external affair, a picture appears for a moment in the air in front of one's eyes - then the precognition or the omen is expansive and will have future ramifications. The biddings of these types of omens have a universal aspect; very impersonal yet personalized to the capacity of the one who sees.

As the influx of information streams through the crown, one will see and know. It is crucial at this point not to speak of what you see for the very essence of what has been seen is a precursor to the real event. So it is imperative to wait when you first see a flower (e.g. an omen) and know that it is only one petal.

You must wait patiently for the full flower to appear. Only then, when it is complete in its manifestation, will one smell the full ramifications of the fragrance that culminates into an event that may be monumental for the ones who are open to it.

A warrior learns to perceive the event silently and as the unveiling occurs through the first recognition, the magic of eternity wields its power so as to be witnessed by the seer. On the other hand, if a warrior were to self-validate, this dissipates the power of the first petal: the first omen seen.

Thus the full emergence becomes distorted and through that very malformity the world reaches out like lead to the eyes of those who have intervened. It is true that all aspects of our self are intertwined, retrieving, gathering and culminating into what will be. Even a mistake of a heavy-handed person culminates into what is ordained to occur.

With this knowledge then, we proceed carefully, without a care. Touch the world lightly with the imperceivable and wait for

SEEKING ALIGNMENT

it to appear as the outcome.

I would like to now focus on the first part of your question. Imagine that we all expand and contract universally like a net. Imagine that each segment of this net crosses over and intertwines with other nets, continually, eternally. As one compartment meets another, recognition occurs. Thus the event hits the individual matrix of each segment, creating precognition.

This all-future, all-present, all-past connectivity cannot be viewed from a linear perspective. It has dimension and these vibrational templates within themselves already know the outcome, by virtue of the fact that when the nets are thrown the indivisible force sees by having each eye unveiled to itself.

As a result of being such a small light in the expansiveness - that is us - many of these compartments are veiled, giving us free will. Yet within all the contradictory terms that can emerge within your awareness there is no free will. There is only the bidding of that which already conceived of what already is. Thus our dilemma.

As we await our path to unveil itself before us we must be aware of one important factor to be taken into consideration. If you stand too close to another, that shadow bears pressure upon your being.

Know that you must move out of its way so as not to absorb the distortion, in essence making it your own through acceptance of the unacceptable. And know that the unacceptable only becomes yours due to the fact that you have allowed someone to coercively shift you to where you should not be. Yet if you have, it is meant to be until you see. Be careful that you are not too late to take notice of what is influencing you.

The ramifications of misalignment bear a heavy price upon one's life path. Moments lost become a lifetime. Then a lifetime may be lost in those very moments.

It is important to realize that the moments we cannot conceive of, in terms of our third eye capacity to interact within dimension, can be seen by a predator that has intertwined within our construct, in and throughout, in a way that is inconceivable yet reveals itself through the very programming that we are faced with.

The failing behind our condition is the fact that much of our destiny is veiled and through this veil this factor that we cannot bring into our calculability can be seen by one who one stands outside of the matrix that is the reality we perceive.

This is a very complex subject and I have spoken extensively about the first type of beings that intervene with our awareness in *The Art of Stalking Parallel Perception*. These inorganics meld with our dreaming attention.

The other inorganic beings are behind everything that is conceivable. Although this sounds negative, endeavor to be who you are and know that what you are may cause a crack or a sealing.

Through an impeccable life one can hermetically tighten one's integrity so that this type of intervention will not occur. It is the very techniques within this book that help seal the openings that we as a humanity have become available to due to the fact that there are forces to contend with on this planet that bear fruit through the hands of our fellow man.

SEEKING ALIGNMENT

As this fruit rots, through its ill intention, see it for what it is and endeavor to change all that is destroying this planet at the moment through removing yourself from negative participation. Consider that there is no time left, for there is not, even though you have your life ahead of you.

THE TECHNIQUES, SERIES ONE: UNVEILING THE THIRD EYE

During these gazing sessions certain changes will unfold for the practitioner. The difficulty lies in explaining what happens versus directly experiencing what occurs through one's own practice. Awakening the third eye has the capacity to dramatically alter the seer and the way the seer acts within his or her life. After delineating the techniques I will explain the ramifications of detaching from the social eddy and becoming aware of the vastness within. It may assist you to write down encounters in order to understand more deeply your shifts in perception.

Technique 1:
The Mirror

Here is where we begin with the first of the gazing series. It is called *The Mirror* and it is an essential preliminary practice to bring awareness into alignment with the intention of gazing.

This is the state of consciousness I was subject to when my attention was redeployed by the masterful acts of my benefactors. As I viewed the complexity that was my compartmentalization in terms of my third eye capacity, I was taught the first technique.

Imagine that you are laying your right hand upon your chest, over your heart center, and choose an object to gaze at. Any will do. Simultaneously view the object while immersed in the feeling of your heart. Realize that, as you see it, it sees you.

Everything you encounter, be aware of the perception that merges with you. You are everything and everything is you, in terms of the feeling that presses from your heart, through your eyes, to what you gaze at.

Be immersed within the union that is ever present, that we have been isolated from by virtue of the fact that our individuality gives us the illusion of separation.

Next, when you meet another human being, view them as you view yourself, while you are immersed in your own heartfelt feelings. This will bring you into a point of union.

Listen to them intently, giving them your full attention, your whole-heartedness. Watch every gesture that emerges. Be careful not to become fixated, even though you are concentrated.

Be without effort, keep a light heart. Do not seek to speak of what you discover. Only listen and watch the event unfold. This is the first step away from the obsessive self. Do not seek personal validation at any point. Do not add any part of yourself.

THE TECHNIQUES, SERIES ONE: UNVEILING THE THIRD EYE

Practice this awareness for at least twenty-one days, until it becomes you. Be of service to those you encounter. Do what they ask of you without quarrel, without question.

Become aware of your bindings, your conditioned programming, through this practice. Remember; do not speak out of turn. Watch and be kind.

Love or honor the other that you are gazing upon as if they were yourself. Give your time to them as if their time was your time to be given.

Do not regret any of your actions and do not seek any form of validation. Do not display any gestures that may reveal the way you feel, if you are being offended. Keep it to yourself.

Grab yourself a diary and write down all the opposing forces and feelings that you have that erupt within you. Do not write about the other person, for in this instance they are you, in terms of the activity you have undertaken.

Move slowly and carefully, gently away from everything. This act within itself will merge and unify you, separating that part of yourself that may be selfish into units that can be examined for recall.

Though this may seem contradictory, in doing this you will begin to become aware of those isolated elements that actually are preventing you from being whole.

This approach has been employed for centuries by monks. Even if they didn't know, they were practicing it. Many of the Buddhist traditions ask the initiate to hold the right hand in front of the chest in a prayer position while gazing downwards at the path that they walk upon, to bring about the awareness of *ascension*.

The Mirror is to be used in conjunction with the first stargazing technique. Not seeking validation is one of the essential secrets incorporated into the recapitulation methods in this book. This and the true nature of ascension will be further expounded upon in later chapters.

Be within your heart.

See and feel with your heart.

Recognize your heart within another.

Speak words from the heart.

Receive the words of another

Within those precious chambers.

Technique 2: *Dragon's Breath*

As you breath in, command your internal dialog to become your breath so that you are without thoughts. Breathe in and out so quietly that you cannot hear it. Be with your heart and your breath and as you gaze upon the world your heart will recognize what it sees, and your breath will obtain the feelings of the sights you observe.

Technique 3:
Stargazing one: *Eternity's Gaze*
Recapitulation Preparation

Eternity's Gaze provides the foundation for all further gazing practices in this series and must be performed prior to all of the following techniques.

Eternity's Gaze must be practiced on a clear night, at a place where stars are visible. You will need to select a primary star with a secondary star attached to it at the 4 to 5 o'clock position. (See illustration on page 117) Once the star is selected the gazer must 'hard gaze' at that primary star. A hard gaze is an intense gaze with minimal blinking.

Keep the small star on the lower right in your peripheral

vision. This is the soft gaze. After a time the prominent star will begin to extend 'legs'. It may look like an insect.

As you gaze at the primary star, you will see that it begins to contract into itself. Simultaneously the secondary star will start to wiggle and will look like it's trying to escape. This will be perceived in the lower 4 to 5 o'clock quadrant of the eye.

When the secondary star finally disappears from your peripheral view, the first part of this practice, and gazing for that night, is finished.

When students visit me the final part of this technique is applied in a specific format. People performing gazing when not in the presence of a nagual must use an adaptation of this method.

After the secondary star has disappeared and the gazing is finished, I walk with the student along the path to their house. Then we turn around and we look at the primary star and I infuse it in their memory. The next day the student comes to my house and I have them sit down and I say to them, "See yourself walking on the path last night with me, at the point where we stopped and looked at the primary star."

They look at the primary star in their memory and I say, "Sit with me here, and from the perspective of the primary star look back down that path, at the time you were last there. Now, how can you be there when you are here sitting with me?"

At the moment of that realization they disappear, like the secondary star disappeared. When not in the presence of the nagual this procedure must be modified. Understanding what occurs between the nagual and student, you may perform the last part of the technique as follows.

On the night of the gazing, walk along a path and look up again at the primary star, then go back home and go to bed. The next morning when you arise you must see from the star's perspective and look at the path where you were the night before, in your mind's eye.

This review will confirm that you are not going to see yourself there, for you are no longer on the path. You are here, where you are sitting. The memory of yourself will become like the secondary star. You will be there for a second, fleetingly, and then you will disappear.

From that perspective, you become the primary star and your image of yourself, which is only there briefly, will disappear by virtue of the fact that the self-image is that secondary star disappearing from the right eye perspective.

A star disappearing is a magnificent thing. Once that star disappears, it will permanently rearrange the right eye's ability to sustain the memory of yourself. The fragmented memory of yourself will fly to the primary star, revealing the fact that you are complete. You are the primary star.

To reiterate: This stargazing practice is completed when you look at the path where you were the night before and from the primary star's perspective you see the path empty.

Watching ourselves disappear is the beginning and the hallmark of our journey into emptiness. It is the beginning of the shift away from the obsessive focus with the self our human form and the social perspective and the initiation into *Eternity's Gaze*.

ETERNITY'S GAZE ILLUSTRATION

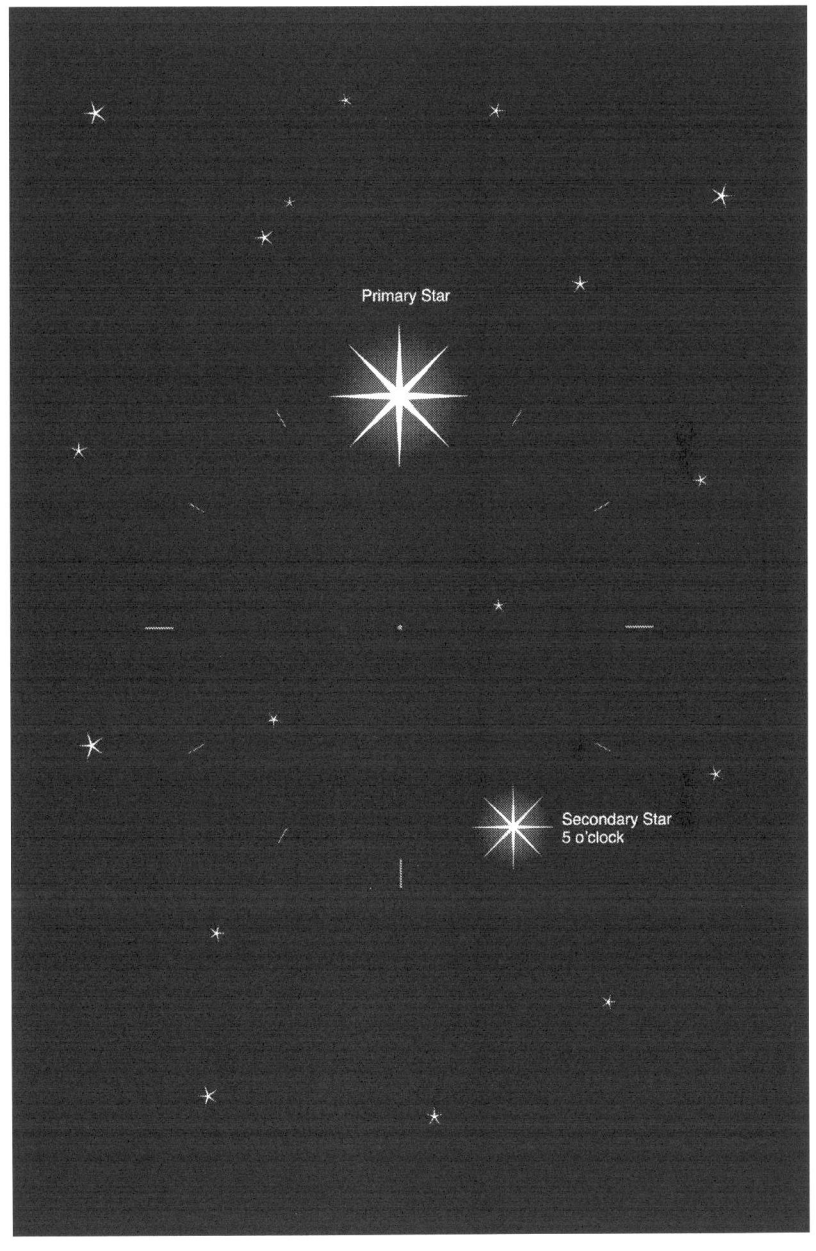

THE TECHNIQUES, SERIES ONE: UNVEILING THE THIRD EYE

LOSING THE NEED FOR VALIDATION

Here I will explain what *Eternity's Gaze* will accomplish for the person who practices it. Performing it once is all that is needed to initiate a transformation.

The primary star represents the self: The seer that steps upon this tangible world. The secondary star represents the reflection of that self.

As the gazer focuses upon the primary star, the secondary star disappears momentarily and then returns. This is the first step to understanding the self and the consequences of the secondary star that attaches itself to the primary.

As the primary star we know, we feel, we hear. All of our

senses are alive, vibrating with the input of the world around us. We are 100% present, yet the percentage of our self that exists beyond that moment of realization has vanished at the instant we wish to conceive of it.

We are existing as a memory. This is our condition. That very reviewal binds our awareness to what was and to what actually is and to what will become available, by virtue of our fixed or fluid attention on the world that surrounds us. When you look at the primary star you recognize yourself in the solidity of its form.

When the secondary star in the peripheral vision disappears, the self that nestles as a memory is given the message that its purpose is futile and that, in the end, these memories will be reviewed and then vanish at the moment of our death.

It is important here to realize that when the secondary star disappears, it shuts down 95% of the right eye's capacity to possess and hoard itself. Thus the left eye is awakened and its potential to permanently recapitulate each moment that vanishes before us becomes available.

Hence we begin to unveil the third eye and avail ourselves to all that is, instead of manipulating what can be in terms of our memories that may encumber the future aspects of our true self to act with the potency of a warrior's power.

As you look upon the world after you have obtained this technique within your eyes, your heart will begin to recognize the pressures of eternity that seek a present realization of the moment that has just escaped us. Then the memory of what no longer exists becomes a feeling that soon learns to speak on behalf of the eyes, and hence our true journey begins.

Here a warrior is awakened to the most potent adviser there is: their death. From this perspective, *all that is* bears true relevance in the moment that we cannot capture nor control. Thus we lose our fear to live. From this point onwards live without regret.

Plant Gazing Preparation

In order to perform gazing techniques you will first need to prepare:

· Two Dieffenbachia

These plants should be tall enough to prevent the leaves being burnt from the tea light candles you will be using. The pots should be black. If you cannot obtain black pots, cover the pots with black, non-reflective material.

There are several kinds of Dieffenbachia. The ones used for gazing are sturdy and grow straight with a strong stalk. This type of Dieffenbachia originates in Thailand, although they are widespread and available in most nurseries.

Be aware that Dieffenbachia are mildly toxic if eaten, so keep out of reach of toddlers. Never gaze at plants with spines or thorns, they are damaging to the gazer. Mulberry plants can be used alternatively. In addition to the plants, you will require:

· 12 to 20 tea-light candles

These should be recessed about two centimeters into the soil. The flames should not be able to be seen directly when gazing at the pots and plants.

Technique 4:
Gazing At One Plant

Once you have everything set up, sit comfortably at the appropriate distance from the plant. Become aware of the play of shadow and light that emanates from the plant itself.

Become absorbed with the shadows that dance upon the wall and the ceilings, looking ahead and allowing your peripheral and hard gaze to be engaged by the interplay of light. Gently begin to notice the empty spaces in between the shadows.

As you do this you may experience sensations in your body: tingling, a feeling of comfort. When this occurs take your gaze to the center of the plant. Do exactly the same as you did with the walls and the ceiling. Focus upon the light and the darkness that emanates from the leaves.

Firstly, set your eyes upon on the most prominent dark leaf and peripherally watch everything else as a visual interplay occurring before you. Then shift your gaze to the lightest leaf and do the same. Once this has been absorbed, familiarize yourself with the quadrants.

Place your gaze on the 12 o'clock position. Rotate clockwise to 3 then to 6, to 9 and once again back to 12. Upon completing your first round, take your eyes to the outer perimeter of the plant, which will be your hard gaze position. (See illustration on the page following the description.) Once you have identified your hard gaze perimeter, go through your quadrants in a clockwise manner again.

The next phase is to return to 12 o'clock and this time become aware of your second gaze, which is your soft gaze, on the corresponding point of the inner perimeter, as displayed in the image by the blue numbers.

As you focus on your hard gaze, indirectly be aware of the plant with your soft gaze. Keep doing your rotations and in a relaxed manner wait for the color blue to appear within the peripheral gaze, your soft gaze.

Do not struggle to see this phenomenon. It will appear by itself. You may see a dot, a mere glimmer. If this is the case then you know that quadrant has been activated. Then move on to the next position in the sequence.

If you have any difficulty finding the blue, bring your hard gaze closer to the plant (i.e. make the radius of your gazing perimeter smaller), shortening your soft gaze. If this does not reveal the blue then increase the distance of your hard gaze away from the plant, thereby increasing your soft gaze perimeter.

It may be that in each quadrant you need to move your gaze in or out. It will all depend on the day, so be prepared to expect the unexpected. The same principles apply to gazing at two plants, though there is more peripheral activity happening in comparison to during the single plant gazing.

It is important to find the blue in each quadrant with single plant gazing before you move on to work with two plants.

GAZING AT ONE PLANT ILLUSTRATION

Technique 5:
Gazing At Two Plants

When you gaze at two plants you are accessing your dual peripheral vision. Two specific things are occurring. The soft gaze is on the first plant and there is a second soft gaze that is on the second plant in the further peripheral aspect of your vision.

The hard gaze is focused outside the plants as you rotate through, and the two soft gazes are on the plants in the periphery.

By virtue of this your eyes will realize what you cannot conceive of, that they hold a dual peripheral vision. This is the way the eyes work in conjunction with the third eye to access dimensionality.

THE TECHNIQUES, SERIES ONE: UNVEILING THE THIRD EYE

It is within the primary plant being focused upon that the gazer will see the blue and with that awareness will engage in moving through the quadrants. The real secret behind the dual perception is that the second plant acts upon the third eye and opens up the dimensional vortex within, even if you don't *see* the blue.

Dual plant gazing uses the same principles as single plant gazing. When gazing at two plants you create an area circling both the plants in which to gaze. This perimeter around the plants will vary in size depending on the individual. Try an area between six inches to a foot. See illustration on page 132.

Begin again by gazing at the center, between the two plants, taking in the light from the plants and then moving to the 12 o'clock position. As you fill your eyes with the light from the plants in the 12 o'clock position, you are feeding the lower 6 o'clock quadrants of the eyes, as this is the area from which you are taking in the light of the plants from your peripheral vision.

Wait until a deep brilliant blue area appears somewhere around the plant; perhaps radiating from the edges of the plant itself, or perhaps just in one particular place.

When the blue appears, move on to the next quadrant, at the 3 o'clock position. Now your eyes are being fed in their left 9 o'clock inner quadrant of the eye.

Again you wait for the blue to appear and when it does move your gaze to the next position at 6 o'clock. In this position the upper 12 o'clock quadrants of the eyes are being fed. When the blue appears again move to the next quadrant, the 9 o'clock position, where the right 3 o'clock quadrants of the eyes are being fed.

From here the gaze returns to the final position, 12 o'clock, and then to the center of the two plants and the cycle is complete. The quadrants of the eyes during this process are being fed with electromagnetic light from the blue color spectrum.

As you move through the quadrants and look at the plants in your peripheral vision you should also be aware of the light and shadows within the room or area being lit from the candles and plants. Avail your awareness to the subtleties within their movements. Notice the edges of the plants. Remember to be careful to move the eyes in a clockwise direction *only*.

GAZING AT TWO PLANTS

Walking the Gaze In

If you experience any agitation or frustration, gazing should cease immediately. You then should embark upon a process called *walking the gaze-in*. Stop gazing, blow the candles out and go for a walk.

Do not engage anyone or look directly at anyone during the walk. This will allow the gazing experience to be absorbed without frustration or agitation. It is important to employ the correct mood for gazing. Remain fluid and without fixation or morbidity of any kind during gazing practices.

Always Rotate Clockwise

Here I must reiterate the need to continue the rotations clockwise through quadrants during all gazing. To go counter clockwise must be avoided *under all circumstances* as it opens a gateway that is detrimental.

A student of mine was performing *flower gazing* with me, a technique that will be elucidated later in this book. I saw a tubular beam of shadow descend down upon the scene in front of us where she was gazing, and when I asked my student if she had just moved her eyes counter-clockwise at that moment she confirmed that she had very briefly done this.

Later on that evening, and for the next few nights, my

student had the feeling of a presence in her room as she slept. Upon awakening she saw that the items on an altar she had set up were being rearranged mysteriously and banged down harshly right in front of her. It took a few days for these intrusions to desist and this was the result of moving her eyes only briefly counter-clockwise.

The Tibetan swastika indicates by the bent arms that all practices pertaining to light move harmoniously in this direction. When the eyes rotate clockwise this locks and stops the influence of the visual context of the construct from entering the right eye, and thereby being interpreted and filtered into one's perception as mind chatter and conditioned social responses.

Simultaneously, during these rotations, the left eye will increase its capacity to rotate anti-clockwise and open to the universe and the world at large, to witness all events in a perpetual state of recapitulation.

This unique rotation allows the seer to harvest the units of information that are pertinent for the moment at hand, sending the gestures - whether they be verbal, physical, or manifest as flares of light emanating from another's body or the circumstances at large - directly to the heart.

These occurrences are to be either witnessed silently as insight. Or, if need be, the spoken word is sent via skimming to the throat center so that one may speak the truth that they have never heard themselves utter before. This will be further elaborated upon as you enter more deeply into this book.

Q: These techniques are very beautiful and feel carefully arranged so that every aspect of the practices has meaning and elicits a potent effect. What is the reason for using dieffenbachia plants?

A: The dieffenbachia by nature are guardians. They exude a most exquisite blue when the gazing techniques are utilized. These plants develop a bond very quickly with the gazer, and when this bond is completed the gazer then has absolute access to every plant within that species on this planet. This is established through gazing at these one or two plants in the beginning. The symbiosis that they have with all their own plant species is amazing.

In combination with stargazing, dieffenbachias are beyond anything I have ever experienced. When they grow to the height of the gazer you can put them inside your front entrance to protect the house. Usually what they do is send out small shock waves to a stranger's body when they enter and the visitor receives a minor jolt, thinking that there is a person standing there.

The other ability they have, by grace of the color they emanate, is that they connect to the third eye of anybody who enters your house without you knowing. They will proceed to send a visual picture as an image of you to the unwelcome person in your house and it will hit them as a picture of your face within their third eye region and shock them. This has been absolutely my experience with them.

When I was living in Bali the person who used to clean our house would constantly ask, "Why am I getting shocks and seeing your face?" and I explained exactly what I said above.

Q: Is the stargazing practice of *Eternity's Gaze* something to be done just once, or to be repeated? Likewise, following the gazing practices in sequence, does that mean to cycle through the series in sequence repeatedly?

A: It is a good idea to cycle through in order. *Eternity's Gaze* only needs to be done once. There is a similar follow up technique that also only needs to be done once, which is called *Equalization*.

Once you have found the blue in each of the quadrants, the rotations are something you only need to do every now and then. If you need to build your confidence keep cycling through, but forcing something that has already happened will not make things occur more quickly. Once you detect the blue a natural cascade will be set in motion.

Be patient. You will unfold in a fashion that is timely to you alone. What will happen once you have cycled through all the gazing sequences is that your eyes will become sensitive to unusual light frequencies that you have never seen before, or more aptly never noticed that you were seeing. Then your journey truly begins.

When I myself gaze into a garden at night, I am pleasantly confronted with spider web-like filaments of light emanating from everywhere. It is a sight to behold.

Q: In the first series of gazing practices there is no mention of blinking. Is it ok to blink whenever you need to while gazing? Or is there a benefit in blinking as little as possible, e.g. to stretch out the time you can go without blinking? This brings up some stinging and tears. I wonder if that is a positive process, like a cleansing of some kind.

A: Just be natural. Hard gaze and blink when you need to blink.

Q: I find it hard to create a completely black space for gazing. I can black out a whole wall of my studio, yet the floor is pale. So I can do the plant gazing techniques in a field of black of about 4m squared, while my vision extends beyond to paler surroundings.

Likewise, if I use the outdoors as a backdrop, it is only totally black during dark moon, while at other times I can see what is there, with the time it takes my eyes to adjust to seeing through the darkness varying. Is this ok for experiencing the full benefits of gazing?

A: No problem. Just set up your area so that your eyes don't directly contact another source of light other than the candles and it should be fine. There is no problem as long as you can detect the blue in your peripheral vision. If there are any reflective surfaces that disturb this, just cover them with black cloth.

Q: "It is important here to realize that when the secondary star disappears, it shuts down 95% of the right eye's capacity to possess and hoard itself. Thus the left eye is awakened and its potential to permanently recapitulate each moment that vanishes before us becomes available."

Could you elaborate on why it is the right eye that is to be shut down? In one possible terminology of discussing it, does it have to do with memory, and/or left and right brain function?

A: It has to do with shutting down the right eye's absorption rate and obviously this is linked to visual pictures entering the inner landscape of the third eye as memories that are then turned into dream sequences that don't bear the same hallmarks as the original memory contained.

This is one of the reasons that a coupling technique to gazing is to command yourself not to dream when going to bed at night, so as to slow down the original eddy that creates the inorganic impetus that is the endless labyrinth of *the second attention*, or dream realities.

Applying all the techniques introduced here will give the warrior the capacity to submit the inner visual imagery to eternity, thus becoming a conduit of that and being of true service to humanity at large, by virtue of foregoing all the mechanisms of control that existed previously.

The functionality of our dysfunctional programming is part of the legacy we have inherited that must be reverted into a new way of being, as has already been expounded upon in previous chapters.

Q: Earlier I asked about the role of the blood in the womb for a seer, however I wasn't seeing a kind of bio-medical function, I was seeing a function of blood and the magnetic nutrients within it playing a role in our awareness, or perception of reality, and how gravity relates to this.

I heard you once refer to gravity being a result of light becoming electro-magnetic and saying that when this is recognized then the scientists of today may truly understand the reality of gravity. Can you elaborate on anything to do with this aspect of blood-magnetics as related to the heart and awareness?

A: When one gazes at a star they absorb light energy. Each star gazed upon has frequency and travels the universe gathering information through each quadrant that it passes through - which pertains to each hundred thousand light years that the light of that star has traversed before it reaches us - swirling like the meridians of the body to arrive at the one who gazes.

This chi, when absorbed by a seer, becomes electromagnetic. This bio-electromagnetic energy then begins to amass and the light frequency gains density, thus the practitioner begins to feel magnetism around their hands and eventually through their whole being.

Light is secondary. Light converged from sound yet the sound itself was a frequency that amassed from all quarters upon itself. When the light frequency gained density all forms began to appear, from the subtlest etheric light to the complexity of a planetary system.

It is not what you absorb on the level of your intellect that is important. It is what you realize from what you have seen that will allow you to peek into the realities that you wish to uncover. So in your journey, as within everyone's, what one wants and what one gets is a reflection of the intent that is their life path that delivers them to the truth, which is a culmination of their personal power in comparison to the universe at large: The great smoking mirror.

And yes, it is true; when light frequencies become electromagnetically denser then the phenomenon of gravity occurs. I know this as a fact by virtue of witnessing on numerous occasions my hands accidentally moving something through telekinesis that I had focused on from a distance.

This density that moves the objects around my body without me touching them creates the reality that is the gravity that my energy field grasps in terms of the object moving.

Technique 6:
Stargazing two: *Seeing Light Fibers*

This technique is performed on a clear evening where you have a view of the night sky filled with stars. This practice is the precursor to *people gazing*.

Lie on the ground looking up at the sky-scape. Firstly, take in the whole of the sky. As you relax, choose a star and hard gaze at it. The star will begin to blink and you will see fibers shooting out a long way from the star. The stars in the peripheral vision will begin to move.

Now look at the next star that attracts your attention. You will begin to notice lines shooting between stars so quickly that they are almost imperceptible. From this point you should shift your gaze to the fibers themselves and follow the fibers wherever they take your attention, not focusing on any star in particular.

As you become aware of the lines emanating from stars you will begin to be aware of the fibers emanating from people as well.

Technique 7:
People Gazing

When you look upon another you look upon yourself.

For this practice you should choose a place frequented by many people where it is possible to gaze unobtrusively.

When gazing at people, ground yourself within your integrity. This can be achieved by placing your awareness on your heart and feeling the energy become enlivened within this precious center. Even though the primary focus is on the heart, this inevitably activates the symbiotic relationship with the third eye matrix simultaneously.

Observe nuances and gestures you are drawn to. You will be

alerted to what is relevant by simply going to what your eyes and body notice.

Using this gazing technique you are simultaneously observing yourself and you will begin to become aware of the subtleties within human gesturing, which will enable you to eradicate superfluous, learned and habitual movements and gestures within your own behavior. This kind of gazing gathers momentum with use and will help you develop the ability to see within yourself.

Information about the people being gazed at may arrive as you practice. This form of gazing should be done lightly, not imposing one's attention on the subjects but being open to the subtleties reflected back at you via your non-intrusive engagement.

For perhaps thousands of years seers have dreamed for the purpose of harvesting inorganic energy, which they required in order to access the third attention. The evolution of seeing involves intending not to dream in order to be awake to *this* dream and thus not be trapped in dreaming by the lure of inorganic influences, which in actual fact was a mere reflection of the original programming.

The power dreamers have found in that realm through the second attention has been both intoxicating and enticing, and has proved to be a significant trap.

Of course at times the new seers will dream but when they do, by virtue of being empty of their intent and their bids for power, their dreams will be pertinent to their waking world, or have specific meaning. The difference is that the new seers' intent is not focused on gathering power through alternate constructs, but is clearly focused in the waking dream.

Every organic being is bursting with its own original inorganic essence, outwardly projected, creating this reality that we live in, even if the object is seemingly inanimate, and *this* is what we need to work with. The new seers are fusing their dreaming energy with their waking reality in order to unify universal attention.

Seers are able to become aware of inorganic energy in the

waking construct through gazing and thereby harvesting pictorial imagery as vibratory units of information to be decoded. Discharges of energy emanate from individuals whose essence is not sealed in their breastplate, escaping as delicate threads of luminosity to be read. This topic is discussed in detail under the heading *Harvesting and Skimming Eternity.*

When gazing at people you will notice subtle light lines shooting between them. Even if you do not immediately perceive this in the beginning, your eyes will begin to shift from one person to another and stay for the pertinent amount of time necessary to allow this visual phenomena to become available to you.

While you notice, as you have always done, begin to become aware that this internal processing alerts a very subtle pressure arising within your breastplate, in your heart center. Do not become attached to this feeling.

As the momentum gathers in terms of you being aware of the pressure applied, you harvest the energy that you have observed. And remember, you have done this *all your life*. It is just that you have forgotten to see what you know.

Do not speak to yourself about the feelings that arise. Hold them gently. Observe them while you observe the environment.

Then you will notice that when you are with other people and you are observing without seeking validation, this original pressure will skim the content of the energy that you have within your breastplate and you will then discover that the harvested influx enables you to speak truths pertinent to your circumstance.

It is a journey of waiting. Do not seek validation. Do not fall into any social ebbs in terms of conditioning. Wait patiently while this joyous pressure builds, and if it is not joyous there is much wisdom contained there within.

Be detached yet fully informed. Proceed carefully and touch the world lightly. When the time is appropriate an internal skimmed flare will shoot to your throat center, enabling you to speak while simultaneously seeing. It is a journey that awaits for one to walk upon it.

When gazing at human entities, you are entering into non-linear perspectives in terms of assimilating time. You will absorb the culmination of that person's accumulative experience - which identifies their consciousness as units of information to be understood - as an indicative feeling pertaining to their diminished capacity to realize that they are socially bound instead of eternally connected.

This type of gazing allows the warrior to appreciate the confines of another's inevitability, in terms of the incapacity to see beyond the frameworks that exist within their cognitive system.

This ultimately delivers the seer to a state of absolute uncertainty: To know that others are encased, thus recognizing that one's own expansion is also bound to one's personal limitations, even if we have experienced limitlessness itself.

THE TECHNIQUES, SERIES ONE: UNVEILING THE THIRD EYE

Technique 8:
Equalization:
Turning off the Right Eye

Firstly do your normal rotations around both of your plants, still scouting for the blue. Three rotations will suffice. Then from 12 o'clock drop your eyes to the center of the pots.

Next, horizontally take your eyes to the center of the left pot and hard gaze at the middle of the left pot. The right pot will descend either to the 3:15 or 3:30 position.

When the right pot has dropped transfer your gaze to the center of the right pot and watch it equalize, which means it visually returns to its original position.

Now gaze again at the center of the two plants and then return back to 12 o'clock and continue your rotations for three more rounds. Depending on where the right pot drops for you this indicates the next stargazing technique that you must engage in.

For example, if the right pot drops to 3:15 then you must find a primary star with a softer secondary star at the position of 3:15. Hard gaze at the primary star until the secondary star disappears. Then the *Equalization* session is finished.

This practice only needs to be performed once. When you have completed it, become aware of your breath. Breathe in slowly through your nostrils. Fill your lungs and compress it softly down into your lower abdomen.

Breathe in. Hold for three to four seconds. Then breathe out gently so as not to hear the breath. Hold the breath out for only one second and start the cycle again.

What I want you to become aware of is that this technique enables the warrior to stop the internal dialog and internal pictorial imagery. Become aware of the whole room as you breathe in, or of the whole environment around you. As you gently inhale, the air that surrounds you becomes you.

Breathe in silently through your nose and gently lift your head. When you breathe out, slightly drop your head.

Go through this cycle as many times as you wish. What will occur, other than switching off the internal dialog and subduing internal pictorial imagery, is that your heart center will breathe in the enormous amount of energy that surrounds you. The byproduct of this is a feeling of comfort and joy.

Turn your thoughts into your breath. Focus your ears on your environment while your eyes are gently closed. Take the weight off your inner eye as you breathe and listen to the world around you. This technique is employed in conjunction with all others for it pertains to the integrity of the heart process.

When you are in front of someone, use this same breathing method, becoming aware of your own heart chakra while simultaneously being aware of the person in front of you.

Become a conduit of eternity. Be of service to that individual and to your environment. Do not seek validation with body gestures or verbal tones.

Be completely soft, or as hard as you need be. Let your voice be unwavering and speak the truth that arises from within and if that truth cannot be spoken, then observe as an unbiased witness of that which passes through you.

EQUALIZATION A ILLUSTRATION

EQUALIZATION B ILLUSTRATION

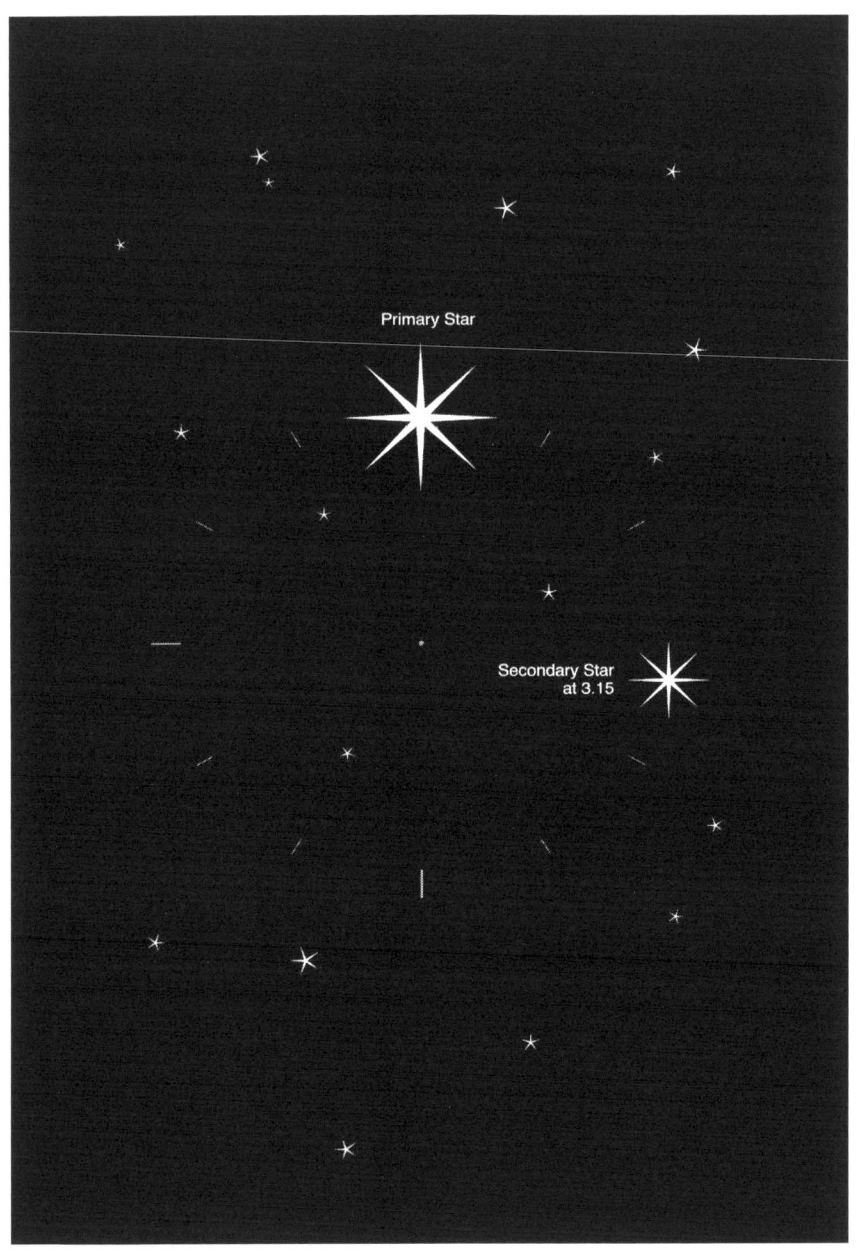

The Swastikas and the Eyes of the Seer

The process of awakening the third eye progresses in correspondence to the heart opening to its true potential within dimension. The third eye rotates on a matrix that has two parts: the upper and lower compartments. The lower part represents the right eye rotation and the upper part represents the left eye rotation. If you intertwine the two symbols, one rotates clockwise and the other anti-clockwise, creating the realities we perceive.

Imagine within your mind's eye that all cardinal points are magnetically connected, both linearly and inter-dimensionally. As one arm reaches toward the other, by the time it comes to the halfway station, the magnetism of the original position is transferred to the next point of arrival (e.g. cardinal axis), thus creating a pole shift which is interdimensional in it's fractalized connectivity to every other position.

This fluctuating juxtaposition occurs with all points concurrently, and thus they all are in connection to where they are going and where they have been. The rotations are so universally integrated, that the true locations of these stationed sites will always remain out of the perceiver's reach due to their interdimensional dispersion.

Now let's look at this from a holographic perspective. Visualize the image of the swastika. The cardinal points seem fixed and two-dimensional, but in actual fact the symbol itself spins on its central axis within a three-dimensional zone.

The right angle arm of the swastika follows the momentum of the rotational force, indicating that the central matrix is spinning. The visual representation of this can be seen as a flag, clearly indicating the direction of that movement. The hub and the circumference are always spinning in opposing revolutions, one expanding outwards and one contracting inwards.

Picture now this form contained within a sphere whose edge is traced by the outer circumference of the rotation, and imagine this three dimensional sphere having a slight protuberance appearing on its periphery that indicates where the arm is located at any point in time within the interior.

From an electromagnetic perspective, this arm is pushing outwardly while the central matrix itself pulls inwardly. Thus expansion and contraction exist simultaneously.

This holographic representation of the swastika that you see is then multiplied to completely cover the interior of that sphere, not only upon the inner edges but throughout all the space in between the hub and the circumference.

Imagine these discs are like spinning coins that completely occupy the interior of that sphere, as positive and negative energetic forces that cannot affix one to another due to the repellent nature of the magnetism they generate; until the universal priority of fixation momentarily intervenes, creating a mandala effect that causes electromagnetic amalgamation.

All localized sites interact interdimensionally with other spheres simultaneously. Thus the universe manifests the immediacy of this connectivity dimensionally, through the harmonious fractalization that this symbol represents, giving an adequate image for those who have not yet seen this phenomenon occurring.

The flag at the end of the arm of the swastika also represents our inability to be on point as perceivers. We lag behind momentarily. This is our condition: to experience the moment that is continually escaping us.

Thus the mystery of one's perception unveils itself at the point where universal attention opens to the eye of the warrior from a momentary perspective to allow them to see that liquescence unfold before them.

When the third eye harmonizes, the natural progression of human consciousness is then fluidly transfixed upon interdimensional doorways that reflect upon every ounce of influx; which is us seeking to see ourselves by virtue of that reflection beckoning us to join it as it joins us; thus neutralizing the perceiver's attention, rendering it null and void and returning it to its origin-less origin.

Within each living entity there exists a point that identifies every sentience as being central to itself. Yet this very identifiable perspective is simultaneously at the hub of every other being that exists within dimension.

Even though fractalization gives the appearance of layering throughout time and space, we are one.

Conceive of this seemingly singular description of a holographic dome. Here we see a symbolic example of the mandala effect, momentarily fixating billions upon billions of awarenesses upon one point within the spiraling matrix of a bubble of perception. Arranged through the electromagnetic polarities that are the filaments - the subtle light frequencies which fluctuate, compensating and relocating via fractalized fusion - this integral cog moves within the dimensional matrices of the realities outlaid, thus defining karmic resolutions, macro and micro-cosmically.

Although this multifaceted process is simultaneously perceived individually, know that within each sphere this fractal anomaly is incomprehensibly complex. And beyond every sphere there are once again billions upon billions - colossal numbers - of multiverses contracting and expanding simultaneously, only allowing entry comparable to the perceiver's ability to alter their perception.

Yet within this inconceivable layering we are unified, eternally one. Some may wish to progress outwardly, some may wish to travel inwardly. Know that there is a point where all existence acknowledges and knows of its complex origins.

SWASTIKAS AND THE EYES OF THE SEER ILLUSTRATION

Q: What is the mandala effect?

A: The mandala effect denotes positive and negative electromagnetic polarities that attract corresponding light frequencies, delivering awareness to the reality of the constructs thus created.

The culmination of the influx of diverse vibrational fields gives validity through that attention to a momentary homogenization that is witnessed by multiple beings simultaneously. In the future the mandala effect will come to be known as the Mandela effect, which describes the changing, interdimensional aspects of reality in terms of influencing timelines, collectively and individually.

Within our three-dimensional construct there are many diverse interactions, linearly and transdimensionally, as embodied within the holographic image of the sphere itself. A seer is only left with one option really: to see, realize and release.

If not, then there is a perpetual loop of avenues of awareness that may indoctrinate, commandeering not only the seer's perception but those who follow their intent. Tibetan mandalas are an organic example of the inherent diversity that we all experience on different levels of consciousness.

Technique 9:
Third Eye Awakening Meditation

This meditation is advantageous to learn before the *Ascension and Descension* plant gazing technique.

Set your alarm clock for 2 o'clock in the morning. When the alarm goes off, assign yourself a task that will keep you fully awake until dawn breaks. Gaze at the sun as it rises, through closed eyelids.

Once you have completed this then proceed to go about your normal morning. Make yourself breakfast. When you are satisfied I would like you to sit down on a comfortable chair. Buy yourself an album of the best Tibetan chanting that you can find, or go to parallelperception.com to obtain a copy of a customized audio accompaniment designed for these purposes.

By virtue of the fact that you are sleep-deprived your body will want to rest. Now what we are activating here is your third eye capacity to conceive of the colors contained therewithin. Your internal dialog will automatically be switched off as a result of the lethargy that has overtaken your body.

Focus all your attention on your ears. Listen carefully to the tones you discern and focus squarely on your third eye region as you look through your eyelids into a seemingly endless blackness.

When the colors are swirling underneath your eyelids, don't allow them to turn into pictorial imagery. Gaze through them and obtain the distance that will engulf you, as if the colors themselves stretch beyond eternity.

Sit silently and await for sleep to overtake you but do not falter. Stay conscious. Remain like this for at least one hour. Then go about your normal day as if you had slept well.

Your body will retain the consciousness that you have

immersed yourself in. Watch everything from this dream-like state and you will find that here is where the third attention, the mystical world of a seer, appears.

Technique 10:
Ascension and Descension

Commence gazing as you would with the two plants. Do three clockwise rotations starting from 12 o'clock, locating the blue. Once this has been completed, your eyes are prepared for the *ascension and descension*.

Upon finishing these three rotations, stop at 12 o'clock and from there drop your focus to the center of the two plants. Gaze intently at this center until white spider web filaments appear. As soon as you have detected this anomaly, directly ascend to your 12 o'clock position.

You may have to go to the highest 12 o'clock perspective

possible, which is as far upward as you can look without losing sight of the plants within your peripheral vision.

Settle your soft gaze on the plants, which will be your 6 o'clock perspective, meaning the plants will be located in the bottom of your visual field. Here you are not seeking to see the blue.

After a time the plants will appear to shrink, stretch sideways, or sink downwards. As the plants descend, be aware of the bodily sensations that occur. At this point the plants are pulling in eternity on your behalf, and allowing universal energy to fill them and you simultaneously. This is the *descension*.

Wait for a few moments and then with lightning speed take your eyes to the 6 o'clock position. You may have to go to the deepest 6 o'clock perspective possible. After a moment you will perceive the plants will begin to stretch upwards and reach toward the ceiling. Here the plants are intervening on your behalf in terms of the *ascension*. Feel the plants ascend as the eyes are gazing downwards.

Keep repeating this process until you are satisfied that the visual anomaly has occurred, thus alerting your body to the experience.

ASCENSION AND DESCENSION ILLUSTRATION

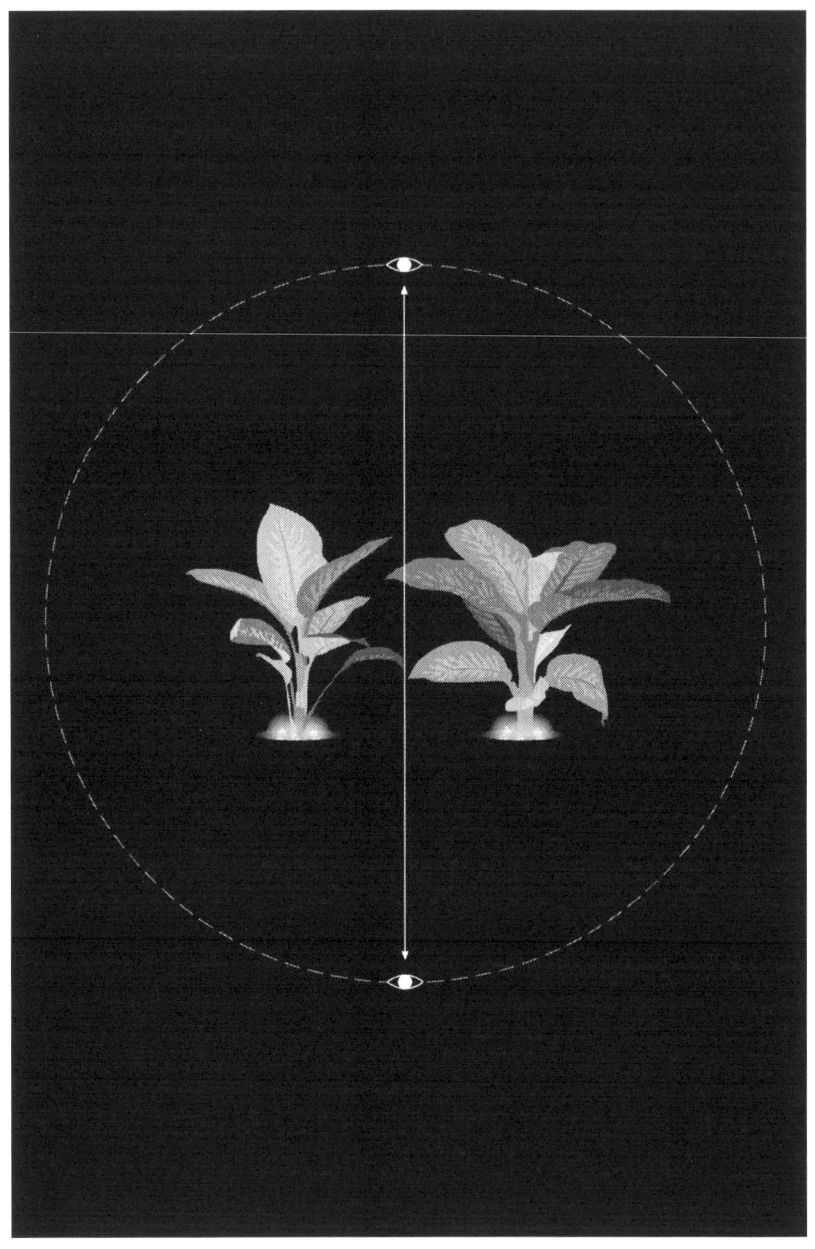

The *ascension and descension* can be seen in various spiritual practices throughout the world. It embodies the way our attention is given or offered to eternity; the way our attention reaches towards the heavens in true prayer, which has been widely misunderstood.

We have been led to believe that when our head is bowed our intention goes within. The opposite is true. When our head is bowed our attention ascends. This is the point where one's intentionality will nestle itself within inner silence. As the silence increases, the function of our awareness will be immersed within this profound emptiness.

Eternity will recognize what we need, not what we want.

As one lifts their head, the inwardly recognized attention couples with the descension of eternity, taking the crucial elements of one's true intent, and delivering you to the experiences that necessitate your growth. The lifting of one's head in actuality has more significance than the bowing. It must be done with as much emptiness as the former.

One knows within their heart what is the genuine truth of what needs to be resolved. It is a bodily sensation that most have forgotten how to act upon, which aligns circumstances to the crucial elements that create the maximum growth. Obviously for each individual this will manifest in different ways.

What binds us all is communal conductivity. Here we traverse, tripping over our actions until we realize that we all must submit to the greater good that enhances the whole and thereby nourishes the one who responds to eternity's beckoning with integrity.

When the eyes are cast downwards and our eyelids fully closed, one's personal seeing is then placed in the third eye, which at that point is inwardly directed upward, opening itself to eternity. As our eyes look down, our third eye looks up and as our eyes look up, our third eye looks down.

Even though this can be seen as a simplistic way to describe the functionality of the third eye perspective, it will allow you to understand one element, which is the process of the *ascension and descension* in terms of their opposites.

The upper and lower compartments of the third eye are like the bottom and top half of a clock face. The entire lower half of the third eye comprises the visions that are seen as the world at large: our daily visual perception. The upper compartment comprises the imagery that a seer obtains through their life path, whether it be internally or externally expressed.

Half closing the eyes allows the warrior to ascend, viewing carefully what pressures their being to observe the influx of that information for review. Recapitulating the feeling without any expectations nor any form of validation, the pressure applied is then sent to eternity to be reviewed and emptied of what originally bound the seer to that which wished to bind.

Slowly lifting the gaze beckons eternity to descend back to the emptiness that awaits within the body consciousness of the empath to be transformed into an impersonal state of transmission that cannot be grasped nor anticipated.

This is true prayer; true acquiescence.

This type of meditative recapitulation is trained through the gazing techniques within this book, via all the plant gazing that employ the 6 o'clock and 12 o'clock perspectives in terms of descension and ascension. When a seer gazes down their empty intent reaches towards eternity. When gazing towards the 12 o'clock perspective, eternity descends.

The most important aspect of this practice is that when an empath receives unbearable pressure from their circumstance they view the images inwardly, with the feelings contained therewithin. Unbiasedly watching this oncoming influx, they seek no outcome, only to witness that which has arrived.

When gazing downwards, head slightly bent forwards, this inwardly gazing perspective will be sent to eternity to be cleansed, viewed by the empty expansiveness of that which cannot be understood.

Thus eternity itself relieves the empath of this burden, to be reviewed on their behalf. Then when the individual lifts their head to the 12 o'clock perspective, slightly raising their chin, eternity will descend back to one's essence, delivering only what will necessitate a clear, empty intention.

While practicing *Ascension and Descension,* be aware of your breath. Breathe in slowly so that you cannot hear the inward and outward flow of that which sustains you. This is true recapitulation: instantaneous reviewal of the moment as it continually escapes us.

Our ability to individually ascend and descend has been manipulated extensively throughout the millennia. Knowledge of the inner workings of this process has been known by few and now will be available to those who inquire.

Visualize this scenario. When you are forced to submit to the will of another, your eyes and your head will slightly bow in submission. As this occurs your very will - your intention - is intercepted by the protagonist, through the fact that they look down upon you. From this hierarchically elevated perspective they will draw upon your ascension, intervening and ascending on your behalf.

Even if the subjugated individual is clear and humble, the fact that they have allowed their bidding for eternity to be intersected by a dominant party means that the will and the desire of the protagonist will take precedence. Everyone has to be extremely careful.

To give an example of this, there was a point in an interview with the Dalai Lama (Ten Questions for the Dalai Lama, by Rick Ray) where he expressed that he wanted to retreat like a wounded animal, to take solitary refuge. The intent of Mao Tse-Tung has taken absolute precedence over his life and the lives of all Tibetans.

It is not that Mao Tse-Tung's power overcame him. It is that the collective consciousness of China subdued his ability to ascend and be free within his sovereignty; thus his extrication occurred. This is not to say that he has been absolutely defeated.

There have been many instances where the misuse of power has enlightened billions of people towards the plight of Tibet. It is the Dalai Lama's individual status that has been interfered with, and this certainly has had an impact upon him and also upon my being and everybody else that has come into contact with this injustice.

It is essential to become aware of this type of corruption in all of its myriad manifestations. It is up to us determine individually and collectively where the controlling factors are in place within our own circumstances, and through that connectivity discover and track the oppression that is applied coercively, which is waylaying our very evolutionary process as sentient beings.

You can see through this example that ascension will be limited to the level of control that is applied by the protagonist. When this occurs the bidding of the dominant factor will then be willfully transferred, forced upon the recipient as their desire.

Through this very subjugation the recipient becomes programmed to believe that the will of another has precedence over their natural ability to govern their own lives. That is how the expansiveness of eternity is denied, through the oppression that misdirects its transmission.

The *ascension and descension,* or the act of prayer, can be manipulated in many, many ways. For example, being persuaded that you want what you don't really need.

Once you learn the ascension and descension technique your innate sense of individual sovereignty will be restored; and if there are enough people understanding this principle, world circumstances will begin to change.

Don't be bound to that which wishes to bind you but be of service. This is so contradictory that you will have to find your way through your own seeing. You can't be told how to act upon this.

When you introduce this practice and your eyes begin to see, you will start to know with absolute certainty who you are and what you are confronted with. Stand firm and witness that which is in front of you.

Collectively we must not give up our sovereign rights to express the inalienable truths that are within each and every one of us, and slowly but surely lift our consciousness to the point that we all begin to say no to what is obviously not right, in all of our circumstances.

You will know and you will walk your truth, thereby not

allowing other people to apply subterfuge to confuse your path. You will see the gestures that culminate to the very position we are all in at this moment.

Protest your rights, not seeking validation but knowing that a silent movement in terms of participation toward a progressive future will unveil greater possibilities as you dislodge the chains that bind you to something that is not correct.

After you have familiarized yourself with the plant gazing and the ascension and descension of the plants you may perform Technique 11: *Meditation to accompany the ascension and descension principles.*

Technique 11:
Meditation to Accompany the Ascension and Descension

This meditation follows on from the *Ascension and Descension* technique, beginning at the 12 o'clock position when the plants start to descend.

As they descend you are receiving energy from eternity, energy from the light source and the shadows. At the beginning you are dependent on the plants to show you this, but this meditation enables you to embody the practice and achieve independence from the plants.

Initially you will need the plants but through meditation will develop your own channels of connectivity. You will begin to receive energy from eternity within light and shadows. Remember that shadows aren't bad. They contain filaments of light. One cannot have shadows without the filaments.

Shadows contain secrets and are the reflection of the plant. They can tell us what others are intending, after we have engaged in the techniques. Your eyes will retain the memory of shadows, thereby re-locating it within your body consciousness, revealing what is concealed in the gestures of others.

When we work with a plant, we work with every single member of that species, since all plants share one source, one plant teacher. The same goes for birds, other animals, and people.

Whatever the species, we share one source. So, as the plants are descending, we are pulling in all the electromagnetic energy connected to all the other plants as well. This energy is light energy, star energy.

As the plants are descending, move your eyes to the 6 o'clock position. As you shift your gaze to 6 o'clock the plants will start to ascend. When this occurs, close your eyes immediately to stop the ascension.

Keep your eyes closed and in the descending position (looking downwards to 6 o'clock), put your attention on your navel area. By closing your eyes, you are stating your independence from the plants.

While your eyes are closed, you will still see the visual imprint of the plants. Use your internal image of this and the color of the plants - it does not matter which color you see - and turn what you see into a ball of energy. Place the energy ball three digits below your navel.

This position is called *Chi hi*, and it is the upper lid of your *lower cauldron,* or *Dantien.* Your eyes remain closed and gazing downward, stay like this for a moment.

Next, you will transfer the ability to ascend. Remember, you relied on the plants to ascend and descend, and now you will do this by yourself. To achieve this, while your eyes are gazing downward and closed and your attention is on your navel area, lift your chin a little, and as you do this see the ball of light rising to your heart center. By moving your chin this way slightly, your head will arrive in a neutral position, with eyes looking forward but still closed.

From this position allow the ball ascend to the mid-eye region by slightly elongating the neck and minutely nodding the head forwards. As the head tips gently downward the ball of energy will rise to the third eye, and you will see that luminous sphere either inside or outside the body in the third eye region.

Now lift the ball from the mid-eye to the crown by throwing the head back slightly, as if you were sitting in a chair upright and began to drift into sleep. That sudden but slight motion – like catching the head before it falls backwards - throws the ball to the crown position.

Observe that when the energy ball arrives at the crown it is felt more like a dish spinning on the top of the head, which then folded upward like a water lily closing at night, resembling a builder's plumb that is pointing towards the zenith.

Now become very still and be in a state of inner silence. If you do not feel this inward quietude do not worry, simply repeat the process from the beginning of this technique, over again if need be, until absorbed in total stillness.

Some will perform this meditation and drop into silence immediately. If this doesn't occur it is not important. Each day our energy is different. Simply repeat the practice until you arrive at this stillness. This allows us to apply the ascension and descension principles independently from the plants.

The plants of course may be gazed upon again, and you and your plants will get to know each other well. Dieffenbachias are protectors and will guard you as they come to know you. But, as with all techniques, it is important that you remain free from fixation, with your energy fluid and without internal entrapments.

HARVESTING AND SKIMMING ETERNITY

Once you have immersed yourself in people gazing you will begin to notice, even if you don't see and know it immediately, that we are all intimately connected by strands of light.

As your capacity to see increases you will become aware of gestures emanating as flares. These flares contain information. They are not too dissimilar to the sight of a candle flame when one looks directly and then pulls their eyes away to look elsewhere. A visual imprint is left. However, this is only a description of how seeing appears to the eyes.

When one notices flares, the inalienable essential truths embedded therewithin are absorbed as caches of information that lead the seer to conclude with pinpoint precision the dimensional content portrayed. As this influx is received by the eyes it is harvested, absorbed in the breastplate; a spinning shield that is the heart center.

When this influx reaches the core of one's being, the interactive aspects of the flares combine with the power of the one who sees, thus giving them the pertinent amount of information to either be spoken or acted upon without words. This becomes the means by which the seer navigates their way through the presenting circumstance.

Many words are spoken that were meant to be walked upon. A warrior learns through trial and error that the self that spoke was misaligned with the third eye capacity to see what necessitates an individual intervention that has the hallmarks of eternity written upon it.

We are meant to recognize those who arrive that have consequence but do not bear relevance to our path. If the seer does not obtain the sight of a flare then they will be alerted by the subtle nuances, which may come in the form of a syntactical response that has verbal undertones or overtones, indicating a primary motive that is being unmasked through the act of listening.

An influx of non-verbal information also arrives and further educates one's body consciousness to the content of micro-gestures, which leap forward unbeknownst to the protagonist, thus putting the empath in a permanent state of alertness, yet at peace with themselves.

Without the interference of the mind one just is a true conduit of that which cannot be known, yet has the possibility of transmission. Whether one perceives from within the social parameters or if one is a seer, in both cases harvesting is taking place.

Those whose consciousness is socially determined are not skimming eternity but are harvesting the regulatory eddy that reinforces their need to be right and to know that there is nothing more to be seen; thus ignoring the influx of eternity via the fact that they are a full cup which continually leaks but is perpetually refilled by the repetitious loops that sustain them.

Activating the left eye anti-clockwise rotation changes that. As complex as the construct here is, the only pertinent truth is that we are beings on our way to die. We are here to be worked upon by life itself. It is how we perceive that work that defines the path we traverse.

As I have explained, the right eye rotates clockwise. The effect of using the techniques in this book is to decrease the clockwise rotation of the right eye and increase the anti-clockwise rotation of the left eye.

Due to social conditioning and the imperatives surrounding this eddy, the right eye rotation is habitually influenced to increase, thus holding and possessing all visual imagery that pertains to the time that we are born within.

The impact of this is to diminish the third eye's capacity to function coherently, through the fact that the influx of false imagery overwhelms a person's ability to traverse beyond the veil; which in this case is the socially determined bandwidth of information that restrains that awareness.

The secondary function of visual imagery harvested in this way is that it is then transferred to dreaming sequences that are said to resolve psychological pressure through the release of events obtained within the first attention, or the waking world. Unfortunately this is not the case.

This type of dreaming sets forth a dynamic that becomes emotionally embedded; an imperative that fortifies itself through strengthening the original desires via the dreamscape. In parallel, this provides the illusion that one's dreams are private, thus magnifying the internal dialogue of the waking person and feeding the delusion that this is also secret and cannot be seen, which in actual fact is very far from the truth.

As the left eye rotates anti-clockwise, this rotation puts one in a perpetual state of recapitulation. What this means is that one reviews their mortality at the moment that it arises. To be immersed in this introspective reflection means one is always aware of the impact of their actions upon the living moment that is continually escaping them.

Left eye rotation increases as one progresses on their path, which ultimately opens up the central matrix of the third eye and crown. This influx of information informs the seer in a way that is external, so they are impacted much more effectively than they were previously.

Harvested perception arrives in the body as knowing. What is seen is uncontaminated by the social milieu. That which is gathered is directly skimmed from eternity and, when absorbed, transforms into truths to be spoken or contained within one's body consciousness, which is skimming the harvested perception.

The person whose left eye is rotating at a faster rate than normal will be available but totally inaccessible. They view the world with the right eye pressing the imagery received outwardly, to be immediately retrieved by the left eye, thus availing the seer to be in a permanent state of reception yet simultaneously absorbed in transmission. And only those who know will notice this happening.

From the emanations that you observe you only obtain exactly what you need to see, thus expanding upon the original body consciousness that arrives upon the scene; not expecting anything beyond the point of arrival that continually escapes the grasp of one who does not want to hold onto what is.

As we progress on our path, the inevitability of our eyes discerns the moment that arrives for the full impact, which is the culmination of our predetermined destinies, to collide. In a normal circumstance, this momentary exchange would create the necessary binding tensions to culminate into events that can be called an influx of information that becomes one's personal path or karma.

It is not the karma, the points of reactivity, that we now focus on. Even the idea itself creates such a sustainable torpor that all is lost in the premise that the word karma evokes, thereby setting up the stage for expectations to provide the impetus for assumptions.

Assumptions lead us where we want to proceed instead of to what we need to realize and what necessitates true seeing, which cannot be led. It can only be arrived upon.

Our capacity as seers is defined by the petal that drops so gently in front of us. Thus we wait for the full emergence of the flower to appear. Even though harvesting and skimming seems to be relatively simple, in its application it is far from it.

As I breathe in while writing these words, my seeing within my heart center, which has been harvested for many years, distinctly recognizes that what awaits me has already been foreseen. This is the third eye capacity to sweep to the four corners, which is my destiny and yours intertwined.

As my breath pulls in I harvest the feeling from the fragments of what I ultimately will perceive. I listen to the sounds that indicate the steps that I will walk and feel the pressure of eternity guiding me to see what I have not yet seen.

It is vitally important to understand that in normal circumstances - under the strenuous ebbs that are the torpor that exists within a socialized environment, demanding our eyes bind with that which *is* - the energetic influx of what presents itself is masked, for it conveys a perspective that has not been seen by those who do not practice the awareness of the unseen containment that contains them.

Here the small bands of light will pressure - through *expectation* - the eyes to spin incorrectly so as to hold fixed - through *preoccupation* - ideologies that pertain only to the willful acts of those that hold the world static in that very eddy through socially compliant expression; solidifying their reality into the limited boundaries that inevitably bind their limitlessness to a tethered field of expectations that is our construct, which we must walk away from at this very moment.

As a seer develops their inaccessibility to the social milieu by being absolutely available to eternity, their right eye rotation is significantly slowed down and their left eye begins to recapitulate continually, allowing them to access holographic information and thus altering the linear process of memory.

When a seer harvests the influx of eternity they obtain an

electromagnetic boost, for their third eye has already traversed the future. And in the moment that the phenomenon are witnessed this awakens the capacity of the third eye to remember that it has already been there.

Thus a seer waits for themselves to arrive as units of information from others that pertain to their path, through the interlinking aspect of the third eye's capacity to have already traversed the life lived; even before the life arrives organically at a position that absorbs the inorganic units of information, which bear relevance to the consciousness witnessing itself as an eternal communion - reminding the soul that they have already been there.

We are what we see.

Q: What are the consequences if I skim incorrectly?

A: If you lose the ability to skim eternity, what you will be harvesting are social prerogatives. This will become a scripted, intellectual process defined by pre-programmed parameters, and you will no longer be witnessing from a true heart perspective.

HARVESTING AND SKIMMING ETERNITY

Q: I am beginning to understand what you are presenting as an alternate way of being. Can I ask you to define it in another way?

A: Eternity is harvested through absorbing the transdimensional essence of what you witness, even though it is an organic occurrence that has made itself available to you. The process of skimming eternity is that you harvest the manifest realities through feeling. This feeling then transports itself via an energetic process; which is the capacity of the seer to witness that very subtle phenomenon by noting the vibratory signature that avails itself as flares.

Once this resonating force is seen by the heart center, then the heart skims through the memory of what is being seen. If not spoken, it will be witnessed, and the clarity of the seer will determine whether it be action or inaction that is to be taken. Invariably it is the eyes themselves that decipher the encoded information that they see, through the medium of the seer's body consciousness.

We are always engaged in the dual process of assimilating

organic and inorganic energy. The fact that something resonates at a different frequency means that even if it is physical we receive its signature on an energetic level.

In the beginning we only recognize the vibratory frequency that makes itself physically available, through the holographic image that is the reality we receive.

Nevertheless, via conscious consensus, we have learnt not to recognize what we have witnessed as a true mystery. Thus reality is relegated to its respective phylum, which ultimately identifies it from the point of view of reason, foregoing the true essential energetic units of information which lie behind it's existence. That is why a seer learns to gaze at everything they see, and not just look.

Q: How do I open myself to a circumstance when I am practicing non-involvement yet absorbing the inorganic essence of what I am observing?

A: Everybody is available to the inorganic influx, whether one is a seer or not, it just depends what you do with what arrives.

Be careful how you proceed. What you pursue may end up pursuing you.

Sit back in silent fortitude and watch very carefully, not adding a part of yourself, yet allowing what cannot be known to make itself apparent without anything obvious happening. The advantage the seer has is that they don't seek validation. This need gets turned off as a result of the gazing techniques.

The initial feeling of lethargy that ensues is the result of the seer no longer being subject to the opiates that drive their initial primary motives, which have been programmed into them as a 'natural condition'.

A seer ceases to be driven by the need for validation and no longer covets the confirmation that may be socially required to affirm their position, even though what is seen *is* affirmative in correspondence to the consciousness enlivened through the realization of that scene.

Q: Can you explain why it is important to focus on our inevitability?

A: Death is a point in time that reveals that our moments have ended. Here we are confronted with our life's visual imagery. Before we journey beyond this threshold, we journey back into what we were and how we have applied ourselves.

This is the moment where we slip into the third attention, using the capacity of the third eye's deposit of DMT to traverse the dream that we have just lived.

Q: How do I know whether my death is confronting me?

A: You will be humbled by your station in life. You will never take anything for granted. You will wait patiently for your moments to arrive and then apply yourself appropriately in comparison to the circumstances confronting you.

Q: How can we define death as a prominent element, so as to be advised by that elusive anomaly?

A: I've just answered this question, but I will further elaborate. When one is purely advised by their inevitability they will wait for the most appropriate moment in our living circumstance to arrive as an internal intuitiveness, which may appear as an image. Or they will be accompanied by a transparent substance that appears to the seer to be viscous; without form, yet containing information.

This substance has been called spirit, but it is true transmission that accompanies the warrior's personal power. It acts independently of the warrior's will, yet is intimately connected to that.

Q: How can I possibly know if my perception is being influenced by my programming, or if I am seeing?

A: The most magical tool we have at our disposal as a living entity is the possibility to see what presents itself, in all its myriad manifestations that are veiled dimensionally within the complexity of their arrival.

Unfortunately it is possible for our eyes to be reprogrammed to grasp reality in a way so as to be totally captured by its solidity, thereby setting aside that magical facility - the capacity to see within dimension – and thus subduing the heart's primary connectivity to the third eye.

There is always a possibility within our present programming that there is still a grain of sand obscuring one's view. Proceed carefully.

In the end we are the sum total of our doings

and we will be faced by those doings at the moment of our death.

Or is it our death in every moment that we live

that faces us with what we do?

THE TECHNIQUES, SERIES TWO: ADVANCED GAZING

The following techniques have various purposes and may be practiced at your discretion. Some are healing, some are for protection and others are for strengthening. In order to use the third eye properly the seer needs to be clear and empty, without agenda.

Gazing ultimately is our original state of being - our connection with eternity - and allows our heart to work with our third eye and direct our actions appropriately as each moment arrives.

This section is less formal in its context, as are the techniques themselves, which may be applied at any practical time and in no specific order.

The *moon gazing* obviously requires a full moon. At any time other than the full moon (or one or two days either side of the full moon) there is a chance that this ascension practice may draw to you the negative consciousness of other kinds of intentions, and this is undesirable. The plant ascension and descension techniques can be done any time of the month.

Technique 12:
Gateway

Gateway is very special in that if any problems arise in your life that cannot be resolved, this technique will facilitate the pure magic of your dreaming awareness to mysteriously change the untenable circumstances, through a gift given to you in dreaming that will clear obstacles in your daily world.

Gateway is fairly simple. Place your plants outside or on a windowsill, with a star around the 10 or 11 o'clock perspective in the sky. The plants must therefore be situated around the 4 or 5 o'clock right eye perspective, relative to the prominent star. The same rotation procedure is followed as with all the plant gazing practices.

THE TECHNIQUES, SERIES TWO: ADVANCED GAZING

Become familiar with the plants. Gaze into the shadows and light that emanate from the candles. Focus on what your eyes are drawn to. Immerse yourself in that attraction until your body urges you to move your eyes away from the experience that you are seeing.

Take your eyes to the center of the plants. Wait for a mist-like appearance to occur. It will seem fibrous, sometimes foggy and web-like. In some cases it has been described as having a pixelated, ghostly appearance.

Once found, directly shift up to your 12 o'clock perspective. Rotate through your time quadrants in a clockwise cycle, never anticlockwise. Do this three times. Once you have detected the blue, you will gaze upwards and slightly to the left to locate the prominent star that you have chosen in the sky, which will be at the 10 to 11 o'clock perspective.

The star will appear to be maybe ten to fifteen feet above the plants, though this will depend on your location. It can be less, but not too close to the plants.

THE TECHNIQUES, SERIES TWO: ADVANCED GAZING

Hard gaze at the star unblinkingly and view the plants in your peripheral vision, which will be the 4 to 5 o'clock perspective of your right and left eyes' indirect soft gaze. You will notice that the plants will begin to shift as the star starts to change. They will become composed of all colors in the rainbow spectrum.

While this is occurring you will notice that the star itself will begin to spread out as if it has legs. It will get brighter and smaller as if pulsating. It is very important to fixate your gaze upon the star unblinkingly until it disappears.

Obviously you will have to blink every now and then but stay mindful to keep focused. The descension of the star's energy will be governed by the plants, which are in the lower right hand quadrant of your eyes.

I must mention here that you cannot wish for what you want. Remain empty. As you pull the light energy down through the fact that you are looking up, it will merge with the 5 o'clock perspective of your right and left eye.

When the star disappears completely it can be gone from 5

to 30 seconds or sometimes it will be gone for an hour. Other times the star will never reappear. It depends on your personal power.

The next step to this technique is to wait for three days and nights for something to be given to you in a dream. For everybody this gift will be different. It will correspond absolutely and only to what you need and not what you want. With this technique I have been given crystals, which in themselves meant nothing in comparison to the circumstance resolved.

Other students who have practiced *Gateway* have reported experiencing dreams where they have obtained something that makes no sense, and yet, when I have asked them to wait three days and see what happens their circumstances usually resolve themselves.

For each of you it will be different. If you do not receive a gift within three days, do the technique every three days until you are presented with a gift in dreaming.

GATEWAY ILLUSTRATION

THE TECHNIQUES, SERIES TWO: ADVANCED GAZING

Technique 13:
Moon Gazing

You must choose a night with a full moon. Gaze up at the full moon, looking directly at it with a hard gaze. Gaze until it feels that the moon is beginning to 'burn' into you.

Next, move the gaze to the moon's periphery. This may feel like a few centimeters away. Hold this for briefly before moving to your outer rotations.

Beginning at the 12 o'clock position above the moon, gaze for a few moments, with the moon clearly visible in the periphery below, then shift the gaze to the 3 o'clock position. Then move on to the 6 o'clock; then the 9 o'clock; and complete the first cycle by gazing once again directly at the moon for a little while.

Repeat the process two more times for a total of three rotations. End the third rotation at the 12 o'clock position then shift directly down to the 6 o'clock position, so the moon immediately begins to ascend.

Maintain gazing at the 6 o'clock position with the moon above in the periphery until the moon begins to worm its way upward, like a snake (employing the same principle as with the ascension and descension plant gazing).

From the 12 o'clock position the eyes should descend quickly, to well below your normal peripheral gazing position. Once the eyes drop like this the spirit ascends to eternity, capturing the moon in its wake and then the moon wiggles up into the sky. There is a possibility for the surrounding stars to shift their positions dramatically when practicing *Moon Gazing*.

Notes on *Moon Gazing*:

The essential purpose behind *Moon Gazing* is to infuse the upper and lower regions of the third eye with the power of moonlight that ascends and then returns to become the power that combines with the warrior as a nurturing heat that will automatically transform in comparison to the magic available to that seer.

There are specific movement forms that are to be combined with the *Moon Gazing* practices, which I have had guardianship of. These sequences were given to my benefactor, the old nagual Lujan, to be transmitted when I arrived in the Americas to a South American man, whom I discovered upon arrival. These forms are now available via private tuition and group workshops. If you interested to learn you are welcome to visit www.parallelperception.com for further information.

QUETZALCOATL MOON GAZING A ILLUSTRATION

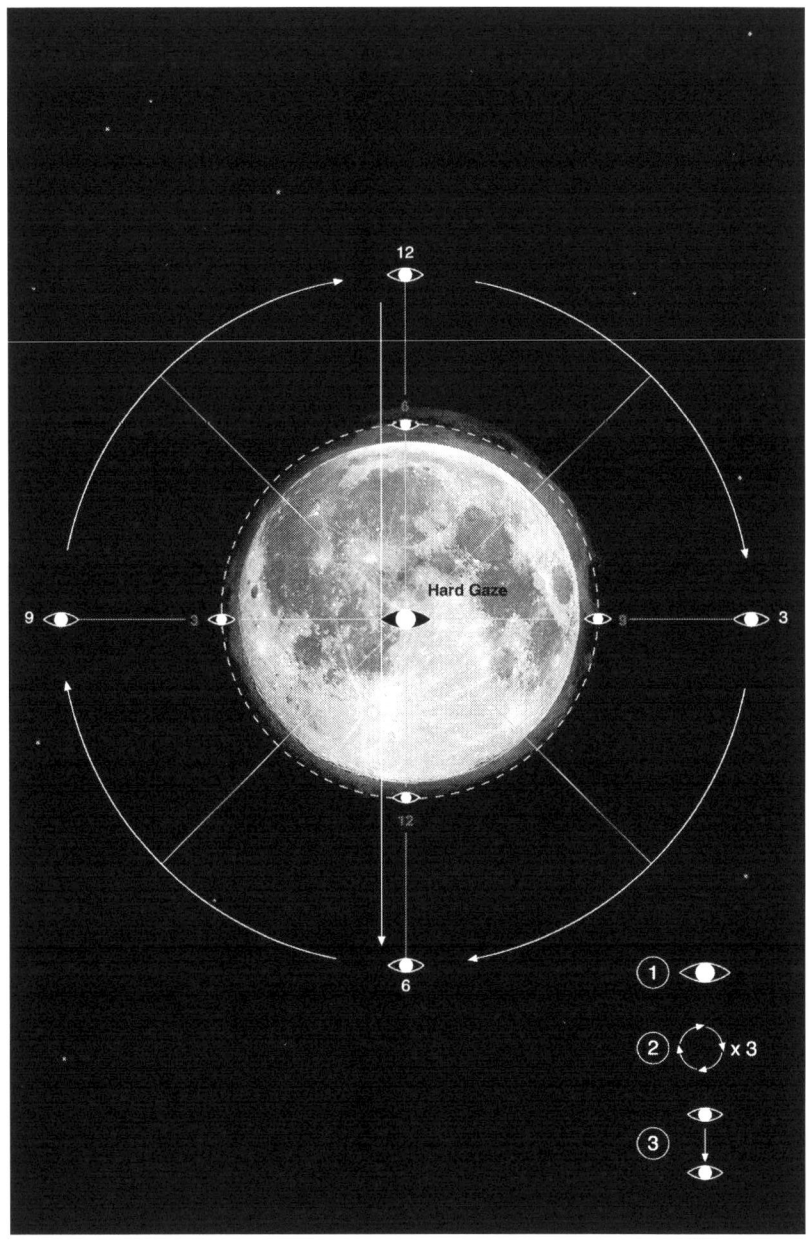

QUETZALCOATL MOON GAZING B ILLUSTRATION

THE TECHNIQUES, SERIES TWO: ADVANCED GAZING

Q: With the *Moon Gazing*, I remember you once said to walk away if nothing was happening after the third rotation - i.e. not to start the gazing sequence over again if one didn't see the moon worm its way up. Is it alright to practice the technique three nights in a row: the day before, the day of, and the day after the full moon?

I practiced *Moon Gazing* last night, not quite aware that it was the day before full moon. I proceeded to go to bed, intending to sleep lightly, and was held within the exquisite image of a colorfully shimmering moon through many hours of my sleep. I would like to keep practicing this if there isn't a reason to not do this.

A: It is best to perform *Moon Gazing* on the full moon only. The waning phases of the moon have been traditionally used for magic, especially the crescent moon. Any portions of darkness that exist beyond the phase of the full moon may have embedded within them undesirable intent.

THE TECHNIQUES, SERIES TWO: ADVANCED GAZING

Technique 14:
Lightning Gazing

Each eye has a blind spot, but this is not the whole truth. The left eye has three rotating blind spots. This is where the eye identifies with the phenomena called *nagual*, or emptiness. It is always there but thoroughly ignored by the consequence of the eyes being absorbed in the image they can see and not what they cannot.

When gazing at lightning, gaze through closed eyelids. As the lightning strikes a bright white circle will appear, a ring. This is exactly that same ring that we are feeding with all the gazing techniques.

Do not turn your head to try to follow the lightning but sit in the darkness with eyes closed. The electromagnetic energy that is stored in the eyes, behind the eyelids, is actually lightning striking. Being in the vicinity of the bolt itself also creates connectivity from the earth, to the feet and the perineum, when gazing with the lids closed.

If the gazer were to practice *Dragon's Tears* while lightning was striking their eyes would be directly struck. You would only see the flash externally even though the internal recognition is occurring. In this case your whole containment field in terms of your skin will absorb the lightning strike.

The primary areas of the body that absorb energy when practicing movements are the bottom of the feet, the hands, mid eyebrow and crown center. As soon as the eyes are *struck* these points are activated.

Notes on *Lightning Gazing*:

The white ring that is seen helps to solidify one's personal power. This is fortifying but also can be dangerous if there are unwanted elements such as arrogance, fear or aggression present. *Lightning gazing* can embed the old habitual behavior patterns and if this does occur it is more difficult to draw them to the surface to be dealt with and cleansed at a later date; either by somebody else or by yourself.

It is important to be formless. If you suspect that you still harbor anger, or coercive, surreptitious characteristics, it is best to avoid *Lightning Gazing* until you are clearer.

Technique 15:
Bone Marrow Breathing

This particular *Bone Marrow Breathing* method is for cleaning and clearing the body. It can be practiced in conjunction with *Moon Gazing*.

Breathe in slowly through the nose and the ear canals at the same time. To accomplish this you must focus your attention on the inner ear as you breathe in. Take a full breath down to the lower cauldron, three finger-widths below the navel. As the breath reaches the lower cauldron become aware of a tingling sensation across the skin.

On the exhale, put your attention on the tip of your nose and attempt to make the sound of your breathing inaudible. Keep mouth closed, lips sealed and tongue resting on the roof of the mouth while cycling the breath. Practice this as often as circumstances permit.

Notes on *Bone Marrow Breathing*:

When initiating this technique, focus on the inner ear and you will feel a cooling sensation as if the air is moving through the ear canal to the lungs. At the point where your skin tingles you are gathering the energy that surrounds the body and absorbing it through the skin. Once you do this enough it will become part of your normal breathing. This type of breathing increases bone density.

The way for us to escape from the encompassing absorption of the living construct is to dissolve our attachments, to relinquish everything that we covet so that we may become the other, the dreamer. Our attachments are the fragments of awareness that absorb us and in essence this is where we partially exist.

In contrast, insightful fragments composed of power are the

whisperings of spirit, the harshness of eternity that crushes the social identification that we deem important.

Each fragment has the power either to expand or entrap our awareness and by eliminating the fragments that are unnecessary or have no relevance we gradually become the *other*, as we let go of that which holds us fixed.

To temper the spirit of a warrior the heart must be open, yet perpetually on guard, to accomplish its task.

THE ACTIVE DREAMER

It is imperative that we intend not to dream, so as to embrace the inevitable evolutionary step that we are meant to take in this present moment in time. Many would question this, and rightfully so. What I am putting forward here is a proposal to sever the magnetic pull that our pre-programming has on our body consciousness.

If you could imagine that our awareness is spherical and from this sphere short fibers of light reach out to a honeycomb maze of awareness, which identifies through each thread–like ribbon the dreaming compartment that we inhabit at the time of our arrival.

Once visited, this site is active continually, utilizing our personal power to sustain itself. It is a multi-faceted event, using many dreaming compartments, even though the awareness seems to be localized as a singular point of reference upon arrival.

Whether we are aware of the layered nature of our dreaming capacity or not, once the neural pathway is established, the habit (which is our unconscious habitual nature to revisit established sites) continues without our conscious intervention, actually mimicking what we do and what we are confronted with in our waking awareness. In other words, we are engaged in our dreams in the same way we are occupied within our waking world.

Because of this entanglement our awareness has been subdivided into a massive neural net that functions seemingly separately to the very impetus of our volition as human beings. When one enters into a dream, by virtue of awaking into that point of reference one has stabilized a compartment for use, which gives the illusion of control of that site.

Thus a portion of one's energy goes into that one localized position, supplying the delusion that the dreamer has obtained the potency of that memory; yet that holographic site has no power to stabilize the living essence of that individual within the waking world, in terms of their own personal potential.

The reason for this is that when we are born the essential essence of our primal imprint is influenced by every entity that enters into our energy field. Thus from the moment we arrive we are being programmed on the level of our body consciousness to obtain and assimilate the artifacts of our predecessors – unbeknownst to them and to our true self.

This patterning inhibits our limitlessness, our original body consciousness, which is nevertheless essentially untouched and which ultimately can't be accessed by the program.

In essence we have turned our back on what we originally were and find it difficult to realize that we can turn around and face this unfathomable part of ourselves. Unfortunately our eyes rotate with us as we turn, reflecting back to us who we are and not who we originally were.

Thus our heritage is our legacy and our legacy becomes our limitation by virtue of the fact that the imprinting is so tightly enmeshed to our inner core that our conscious awareness cannot discern its original emptiness. For our emptiness is so non-invasive compared to the elements constructed around that primal body consciousness.

Through social programming the eyes are aligned to look forward and lose the ability to fully recapitulate those early moments of our existence. One has to forget oneself to realize where the original impetus of their consciousness arose, and this cannot be conceived of through the ways and means of the cognitive system that organized the initial edifice; our legacy. Thus our dilemma as dreamers: to be incapacitated to such a degree that we cannot see the very point of our origin.

That is the reason why it is so important that a warrior no longer seeks validation or recognition for their achievements. For that same construct that builds the idea that needs to be validated is the primal source of illusion that blinds one's sight, through that very need for recognition.

True recapitulation is arrived upon by seeing the truth - that the seer has been caught within the programming - and by letting go of the need to reaffirm that which identifies itself through self - reflection.

When a warrior does not seek themselves, they receive others instead. Through this process they will begin to eradicate the singularities that are the catacombs, the dreaming awareness, which fortify indirectly the attention that sustains their sense of immortality; their need to be validated; or their *legacy*.

Once this shift occurs, the awareness that has been allocated to the deep and profound process of dreaming is then drawn to the surface to act as a voice to be spoken by the seer, until all the singularities unify into their original body consciousness: a silent entity that just was, before we became what we are.

If you truly intend to go beyond who you were, you must embrace the diversity presented by your body consciousness. By doing this you will be faced with the most intense recapitulation that ever could be embarked upon. It is the point where you had arrived but were not aware of it.

Our task is to become aware of what we were before we became what we are. For those of you who have learnt a traditional recapitulation method, allowing your life events to spontaneously reveal themselves and arriving at non-sequential realizations is the first step. Methodical recapitulation isolates events as particularities in terms of life sequencing.

Intentional dreaming reflects exactly the same principle. One becomes engaged in a never-ending loop that is defined by the pre-programming of one's initial circumstances of arrival on this planet. Thus it is a dead end street.

What I am proposing here is that one does not dream. This will create a circulating wheel that surrounds our awareness. How this works is that when one falls asleep they intend not to dream, without a word spoken to themselves. It happens through the intent of the body.

The original body consciousness defines itself wordlessly, then the dreaming compartments slowly drift outwardly until the dreamer's awareness reaches into emptiness, by virtue of the fact that there is nothing to grasp due to the enormous amount of space that is created by the intention *not* to dream.

Now, imagine that the central hub is your awareness, and that there is a wheel spinning around this empty axis. When you don't utilize these compartments for dreaming then they simply become the internal or external imagery of the seer – their third eye capacity to traverse the ever present moment that is continually escaping us.

Instead of these compartments being composed of dream images they will slowly obtain your life path's pre-determined destiny, which will be randomly presented to your third eye as visions – firstly internally and then externally – and this will include precognition, either in dreaming or in waking.

Thus the journey of the empath begins by entering dreams with the intention of not dreaming, to envelop the very consciousness that constructs a world with nothing but silence.

When this vast quietude is reflected back into the eyes and then into the world in which you awaken, the power of that silence interacts with the construct that is a direct reflection of emptiness; thus endowing the warrior with the ability to see the transmission of eternity manifesting as the magic of its symbiosis with us as living beings. This may involve unexpected phenomena such as forms of spontaneous telekinesis becoming apparent.

The seer's attention will become the intent of eternity and then, if their power is sufficient they will know when these transdimensional anomalies occur, acting upon the universal force they cannot possess.

The first thing that you may experience before the full-fledged manifestation of these newfound capacities appear is that you will feel the waxing and waning of another individual's internal attention, as if you are being touched by the feelings projected.

Even though it may seem that the person exuding pressure is enacting a kind of willful gesture through the very subtle element of impacting you emotionally with their feelings, to identify this is not the point. It is the ability of the empath to recognize the energetic imprint of another individual on an etheric level that indicates the first step of becoming aware of the internal process of telekinetic interactivity occurring.

Another thing that may arise is precognitive déjà vu; the ability to see what is contained within another human being's energy field. The list of possible eventualities goes on and on, yet these phenomena are quite different to what you will achieve if you enter into dreaming with the intention to control and search for power inwardly.

The magic of dreams is alluring, yes, but the potency of that realm is only a reflection of the desire of that dreamer. We are not too dissimilar from the animals that surround us. They dream too, yet they cannot consciously intend not to dream. It is merely the DNA expressing itself.

We are more than this. We can intend not to be our program: to walk without expectation and to know what the universe sees at the moment we need to see it.

Q: I would like to ask about the upheavals experienced as a result of the practice of not dreaming. I don't know about others, but for me it has been a very rough ride from the very beginning.

Whenever something shifts toward an emptier state I get crushed by emotional pressure, which sometimes doesn't even feel familiar to me at all.

Simultaneously, my capacity to 'bounce out' and shake off these states has increased dramatically as well. It's like getting violently shaken around. Whenever I understand anything it has suddenly changed... it feels endless. I guess I just wonder if there is any way to understand what is happening or why it's occurring.

A: As with any movement away from a familiar, comfortable state, there will be pressures or upheavals experienced. If someone's original patterning leaves them to be sensitive then their vulnerability may be the most dominant factor for a short period of time.

The world we live in at present has a particular harshness to it. When a seer becomes more aware they feel infinitely more, in terms of what surrounds them. To come to terms with this, in the beginning, *is* the journey that unfolds. We have to take responsibility, and sometimes this is uncomfortable.

Q: Is there anything you can explain regarding how we are being dreamed and, in relation to this, how we function as compartments of the shared dream?

A: We are all intimately connected. As we evolve the higher frequency that becomes available to us manifests the realities that allow us to interact with more potency than the previous consciousness could accommodate. It will only seem that we are the same. Others will view a seer from their perspective, only drawing on the conscious conclusions that are available to them at that time.

To be at our source is to become aware of the origin of our being. That origin expresses itself through the spirit of our awareness. If you go back into the description of compartmentalization, you will begin to understand the answer to your own question, in terms of its complexity.

Q: Reading information about different brain wave patterns, particularly the delta wave pattern, reminded me of intending not to dream. Would it be right to say that this state is a delta state brainwave? It felt like there was something there within the definition including "Access to unconscious and collective unconscious mind".

Are we, by intending not to dream, taking away the emphasis of the brain from mental activity and the self, and allowing it to reach back to the source through delta waves? I found a chart, cruising the net, which helped me visualize the said brainwaves as an interconnected helix. Can all occur at the same time?

It seems that as we are socially programmed to operate we fall heavily on Alpha and Beta, and sometimes on Theta as dreaming, yet that is also deeply enmeshed in the activity of the former two. Does intending not to dream help entrain us to delta waves?

A: Yes it is a Delta state that is entered into when performing the art of intending not to dream. Alpha and beta states are accessed in the waking world as part of our primary functioning as intelligent beings, in order to interact with the elements of the construct that confront us at every moment.

There are those whose body consciousness has integrated

the Theta brain wave pattern, in terms of alignment, by engaging in rigorous practice of various disciplines to stabilize this frequency.

Here consciousness acts on its own, without the intervention of mind. This brain wave pattern is experienced as a form of freedom and elation, where one can intend positive outcomes and learn to use their skills of manifestation within their life.

While this is advantageous, if transferred into dreaming consciousness, the attention will remain enmeshed with Alpha and Beta patterning. One is then faced with another labyrinth that aligns with the living construct and is remixed into endless catacombs. Thus the dilemma of the old seers: the quandary of not being able to find freedom through their dreaming awareness.

Once the warrior reaches this particular stage they need to let go and learn to intend the unintentional: aligning themselves with a higher frequency and allowing their steps to be walked in this world through the manifestation of spirit, which is the direct expression of eternity.

Even though this state is similar to the previous attention obtained, where all things are seemingly possible, it only appears to be the same, in terms of manifestation. But it is not the same.

It is the wordless - walking on the words that are spoken by the seer - that manifests the unmanifest, as a continual delight and surprise, through hearing what is being spoken as if for the first time. Eternity whispers through the seer as they utter the unknowable to one who inquires. The most magical manifestation is that which appears and retreats to its origin-less origin

For this to occur one must be in a very deep brainwave pattern beyond Delta, which I have heard now is being called Epsilon, where there is no reflection of self, no import of 'I'. Even though it appears from an onlooker's perspective that 'I' exists within the seer, it is simply that the emptiness cannot be seen when the seer appears in concrete form before those who witness.

Due to the fact that there is such familiarity with these three brain wave patterns in the daily world, it is not uncommon that these identical patternings are then taken and traversed in dreaming, entangling awareness in limitless combinations and thereby creating a labyrinth for one's dreaming attention to be focused upon.

Once the dreamer attempts to track these seemingly unlimited possibilities they are left with a predicament in terms of trying to retrace their steps of the previous night to establish a dream construct that becomes their point of reference and thus entry.

The quandary is that the stabilized dreaming position is an illusion, which bears similar hallmarks that give a visual referencing system in terms of familiarity with what was previously visited, yet is not exactly the same.

The energy of the warrior has to then adjust to that disparity and through those minor adjustments life force is lost. Flying through the eye of the needle becomes impossible if the thread cannot find the source of that gateway.

By virtue of the fact that the dreamer is accessing the illusion of self from the waking construct *and* the illusion of self in the dreaming construct, in each reality the warrior is faced with the inevitability of their projections in terms of sustaining elements of who they are and what they want, instead of releasing themselves to receive what they need.

This is why it is so crucial not to intend the need for validation within the waking world, so as to witness reality in the fullest spectrum that one can be aware of while simultaneously forgetting oneself; thus being of service. Being immersed within the Delta brain wave pattern, body consciousness transcends limited realities and one becomes subject to intention-less intention.

When this rarified state is then transferred to dreams as a dreamless state, the warrior is delivered to universal consciousness, the basis of all existence. Here is where all manifests from nothing. When this occurs the intuitive empath becomes the central hub of a wheel that has no spokes. All dream images then are transported to the third eye capacity, as a greater wheel rotating around the axis with a vast silence pressing it outwards from that central matrix, the source point itself.

From here the random universal element of the third eye crown capacity intervenes and the warrior becomes a conduit to the spiritual aspect of eternity. Thereby empty intent, though seemingly individualized, caters to the capacity of that seer as they act within the world through their unique configuration.

To intend into the realm of the unintentional (as dreamers have been doing for millennia) has consequences in terms of the entanglement of dreaming attention upon the waking world, and vice versa.

For those of you who have intended to dream, the only thing that needs to be remembered is that the spokes that manifested in the wheel are a mere illusion that need to be dissolved through a practice that is non-dualistic.

Our imminent destruction as a species is at hand. Come back to this world and live one hundred percent in the reality that is fragmenting and falling apart before us, before it is too late. It is here where you are needed, to be one hundred percent conscious of all the mechanisms of control and the destructive force behind those mechanisms. We all must learn to see the devil in the details. We must be with what must be done and stop doing what we have been doing.

Q: Would you consider Delta brainwave entrainment meditation CDs to be beneficial for a warrior? Or is that completely different to accessing that state by one's intention alone?

A: It can be accessed by one's intention alone and the entrainment CDs are also useful to accelerate the process.

Q: As I notice body consciousness awakening I have found that the feelings of those around me mysteriously transfer to me exactly as if they are my feelings. Often they are sensations of blockage or discomfort that seem to be associated with whatever it is that people are hiding from themselves internally.

Is this normal? How can I best bring my attention to a perspective of acceptance of what can often feel like an oppressive limitation in terms of interaction with people? How can I locate my own responsibility in this as a perceiver?

A: Yes, this is normal. Don't seek validation on any level

whatsoever. Reduce your identity. Don't take it personally.

Q: When one is asleep and not dreaming, what happens to body consciousness? Is any consciousness present, such as the formless void or the *clear light* described by Tibetan Buddhists? How do dreamless sleep and body consciousness inform each other?

Is the body consciousness essentially an awareness of the void? If so, is it still aware during sleep? Can you say anything more about how the awareness of the void affects the energy of the waking state?

A: When the consciousness of your body reaches very deep Delta states or Epsilon patterns, your electromagnetic field will embrace only what is appropriate in comparison to your need as a light being.

When immersed in this void-like state, body consciousness assimilates the unknown fractalized essence of eternity in comparison to the light frequencies available, relative to the seer's consciousness at the time of arrival. There is one more stage on from non-existence that I've not yet spoken about.

Within the state of non-being there is a pin prick of light that is like a needle in a haystack. It is very difficult to perceive, but once located expands into universes upon universes of light filaments that once again have contained within their diversity a point of reference that is difficult for the perceiver to locate in the beginning. It is also a pinprick, of darkness, that is non-locatable yet becomes available when consciousness ceases to be.

To answer your question about the awareness of non-being - or the void - affecting the waking state, the most prominent effect is extreme detachment that is intimately connected to everything that exists.

Q: Why do you promote not-dreaming?

A: We need to bring our energy body or light body or double into this realm. In the eventuality of a major shift in consciousness it is imperative that this aspect of our self accompanies us within these transitional times.

To clarify what this really means, by not dreaming the

intention of the warrior's dreaming capacity will expand upwards from their central core, providing vast amounts of inner silence to occupy the space in between their compartments.

When this silence amasses enough power, the compartments then transition back to their original state and become the third eye conductivity sweeping the universe, proceeding harmoniously, projecting forwards and backwards and intertwining multi-dimensionally within our capacity as light beings to traverse that very matrix that has been veiled by virtue of the fact that dreaming had taken precedence.

When this third eye ability attains its ultimate potentiality, the double, which has been known as the dreaming body, will station itself centrally within the physical form of the warrior, within dimension; bringing forward the whisperings of eternity to be expressed as ineffable truths that are not only a welcome surprise to be listened to by another but are also a source of wonderment to the seer who is in reception of that phenomenon as an absolute delight and wonder, hearing their own voice and knowing that what they hear they have never spoken before.

When this particular power fully gains its gravity, the matrix of the third eye then evolves into a very unique functionality. What occurs at this point is that the third eye projection will contain the upper portion of the seer's body as a holographic emanation that then has the capacity to teach individuals multi-dimensionally.

In my own case this has been experienced by my students as them seeing me arrive as a holographic image, not in their dreams but in their waking world, either merely witnessing them or instructing them in terms of what is pertinent for their evolution at that moment in time.

This phenomenon still has attached to it the original veils that the third eye capacity has embedded within its matrix; to forestall these memories flooding in dimensionally as an overwhelming factor that the seer would have to deal with. Consequently, the teacher may not remember all the visitations, yet when this power is established, multiple transmissions do occur.

When this threshold is reached the double or the dreaming

body is no longer randomly utilized as a projection. It becomes forth dimensionally located within the central matrix of the physical body. This is when the third eye capacity becomes fully operational as a teaching tool for many; not only for transmission but as a receptor site to receive information from higher light beings.

Q: Why do you only see half of the body of the third eye projection?

A: This is something I cannot answer, I just don't know. Usually when something is seem there is a pertinent amount of information within the visual matrix of what is recognized. In the case of the double and the third eye projection there are elements of information that remain out of a seer's grasp.

Q: What do you mean when you say that the dreaming body is no longer used as a projection?

I can answer your question in two ways. Firstly, when the seer becomes aware of the double, its eyes look upon the world, providing a second perspective. When this second perspective fully manifests, somebody else witnesses the seer's double appear in front of them, not knowing whether they see the energy double or the physical body. If the seer is in close proximity, this is usually confirmed when they arrive into a room where their double has already appeared.

At the point of physically entering the location, the seer's double vanishes, shocking the person witnessing this rare event. The seer will know what is in the room before they enter, as an intuitive, precognitive visual anomaly, by virtue of the fact that their double's eyes have already seen what has transpired.

This is a simple training method that eternity applies to the seer before their third eye capacity will be fully awakened to act within dimension. When this occurs the seer becomes cognizant that they have developed proximity in comparison to the double and that it is very close to merging within the central vortex of their being.

There have been sorcery stories where the double has appeared in different locations in comparison to the physical body. I can corroborate this myself. On numerous occasions people have reported seeing me appear at great distances from my geographical position.

Stories have been passed down from teacher to student of instances where a powerful shaman will operate from two different locations. It has not been my experience to have the capacity to consciously operate from two places at once.

What I know is that my double has gone from being a great distance away from me to relocating itself within the central matrix of my being – thus endowing my third eye with the holographic potentiality of being in multiple sites at once.

Yet this operational hub still has the same rule applying to it in terms of not being able to completely track and remember every event that has taken place. One does not know where one has been until they arrive where they were, even though where they were has already occurred in comparison to where they are.

This awareness is usually delivered to them via the appearance of someone who has witnessed being taught but who does not remember the full details of what has been transmitted.

The seer's eyes walk upon the previous transmission, giving validity to those teachings within their words and enabling the heart to speak the path that has already been traversed.

To reiterate, this facility manifests in terms of the student finding themselves in the physical presence of the seer, who delivers them the pertinent amount of information in terms of a spontaneous vibrational alignment occurring.

This very resonance then alerts the subtle frequencies that activate the heart to speak the hidden truths that have arrived upon that moment, which have already been transmitted to the student, yet were not remembered until that point of arrival.

This is one of the greatest mysteries, regurgitating the hidden event in a heightened state of awareness that aligns through the frequency already absorbed via a transdimensional teaching.

Vibrational alignment is how one recognizes the auspiciousness of the moment arriving and this is the way that the Tibetans find their lamas: souls that left the living matrix and once again re-entered in another body. It is not re-incarnation, per se. It is simply our ability to move within dimension until our tasks or our destinies fulfill their imminent potentialities.

Once we begin to realize we are dimensional beings and understand the extent of our compartmentalization in terms of its accuracy within fractal interspersion, it becomes possible to discover a departed soul re-entering our earth matrix.

Déjà vu, Premonitions and Omens

Like the wings of a butterfly, déjà vu is a rare and delicate event. When we observe their appearance alighting upon a flower, we immediately notice their wings opening and closing harmoniously. We become aware of the intricate details, yet cannot completely absorb what we have seen.

The seer detects a portion of the pattern that appears momentarily, which immediately shifts when the butterfly transfers from one cardinal point to another as it absorbs nectar from the flower, it's source; thus changing the original visual representation to impact the seer's eyes from an alternate perspective in terms of the patterns upon the wings that were originally presented for observance.

As the wings unfold to the seer's eyes, we begin to recognize the non-sequential intricacy that has made itself available. Omens, whether their manifestation be visual, auditory, olfactory or in the realm of feeling, are mere markings that follow a predetermined non-sequential event that cannot be rationally tracked, yet which is identified through acknowledging the factor that has appeared as an indicator.

This is really the first point that must be recognized, and at the same time ignored, so as to allow the unfolding of what is to come as a universal patterning that presents itself to the eye of the seer.

One of the facilities of the third eye has to do with its connectivity with the heart center. The primary function of these two chakras is the ability to have sight. The heart knows through feeling, yet that feeling is seeing. The third eye sees, yet it is veiled.

When one has a premonition or sees an omen, what arrives is to be observed carefully. There must be no indicative gestures towards that manifestation. It is neither the premonition nor the intuition that is of primary importance. One must watch this event and let it unfold. From a discreet distance the true indicators surrounding the omen itself come to the surface.

Déjà vu is not about us validating our own abilities to perceive in non-ordinary ways. It is a cue that the events unfolding should be witnessed carefully. What is happening in the world right at this time is what is important. And of equal importance to this is our need to witness and not tamper with events as they present themselves. That which will come to pass will have significance for the seer in one way or another.

Watch the world open without interference. In this way we may meet, through the intertwined fabric of the universe. When I encounter certain people, I know we have met before. Certain events are connected through this fabric, through compartments of perception. They will unfold as they should and we must endeavor not to interfere with that process. To be caught up in looking for omens is the same as being trapped by the second attention. It is not the way of the new seers.

If you have a déjà vu experience, it is something you see but cannot entirely remember - so you are meant *not* to act upon it.

You are meant to see it and wait for it to manifest and *then* proceed, although you may have no idea of the outcome in terms of life path directives. Wait for that pre-determined event and remember what you have glimpsed, in terms of your seeing.

Upon that moment you cannot speak of what has been transmitted. The indication is only for your eyes, unless it has been seen communally by another simultaneously. Even then it will not be spoken of because of the recognition that occurs. Move definitively, touch lightly, open your eyes and watch with silence.

Technique 16:
Flower gazing one

Flower gazing is a great way to become aware of the blue spectrum, as petals emanate the blue frequency more efficiently than the dieffenbachia. The reason I introduce these practices after the plant gazing is that they are infinitely more dangerous, as I will explain later.

Light colored and fragrant flowers are used for *flower gazing*. Frangipanis are ideal. Do not smell the flowers collected for gazing purposes.

For this practice you will need:

- A very dark (black or dark blue) backdrop that does not reflect light

- A medium to large fish or flower bowl, big enough to place another glass bowl inside

- A stand, at eye height

- Tea light candles

- About six bunches of frangipanis

A glass bowl is filled to half or two thirds full and frangipanis are floated on the water within the bowl. The smaller bowl is floated on the water in the middle of the frangipanis and has a tea light candle placed in it. The candle flame must not be seen through the frangipani flowers.

The bowl is placed upon a stand at a distance of 8 to 12 feet or so from you, at eye level. The backdrop is arranged behind the bowl so there is no light surrounding your gazing area.

First gaze at the center of the bowl. A patch of brilliant blue will appear above the bowl. Wait for the blue to appear and then begin the rotations from the 12 o'clock position, now gazing at the bowl with the peripheral vision (with the hard gaze from 10 to 20 inches from the bowl or at a distance based on your previous gazing experiences).

Wait at each position for the blue to appear before moving to the next: 3 o'clock, 6 o'clock, 9 o'clock. Always in a clockwise rotation.

Through this technique you are feeding the quadrants of the eyes, as in the plant gazing series. Whilst gazing you should feel the room around you and be aware of the movements of shadow and light, which will often seem enlivened through the gazing process. Remember, never gaze in an anticlockwise direction.

Notes on *Flower Gazing*:

When one of my students first performed this, she said that she saw my face come toward her abruptly out of the circle of blue as she began gazing. It was so immediate that it startled her and her body jumped. I explained that this was because frangipanis are familiar with me. Also these flowers magnify the intent, or the voice, of the gazer.

The intent of the seer is enhanced by the number of petals, which is why frangipanis are used. This is a powerful gazing technique, but is softened by the water used in conjunction with the flowers.

Flower gazing is very good for allowing one to see the blue spectrum. My student asked me why *flower gazing* was not introduced first, as it helped her and others recognize these particular light frequencies. It is precisely because of the ability of the frangipani to magnify intent that it could not be used in the beginning.

In many indigenous communities that practice magic the frangipani is revered. The reason for this is that their flower petals can obtain the inner voice of the practitioner. I will proceed to explain this, not to give value to these old methods, but to allow you to understand why the power of some flowers is more potent than others.

The single frangipani flower has five petals. This number gives the power of etheric transportation. The petals themselves do not intrinsically have a voice of their own; they absorb the voice of the one who wishes to transport their intention, thereby multiplying it by five times.

The petals receive and transmit these inner intentions, and this power of the transportation is wholly and solely dependent on the fragrance of the plant, which will carry the will of the practitioner. If a flower is picked and the fragrance is experienced through inhalation, the very potency of that flower bud will be lost. That is why it is imperative not to smell the frangipani if you wish to use it for magic.

Here I will say that it is not my aim to teach this method of incantation. My desire here is to establish for you the value of gazing at a bunch of frangipani with only the intention of seeing the blue spectrum. This will endow the practitioner with the desire-less desire to know and to receive that which is pertinent to what naturally unfolds, and not to intend the unfolding of something that is not natural.

Many communities that practice magic with the frangipani add their thoughts as desires, as an end to a means. They place the frangipani stem between the index finger and the middle finger of the right hand and rotate it clockwise, wishing for a personally beneficial outcome.

If the flower is rotated anti-clockwise, it will activate the lower regions and be damaging to those that are intended upon. If during this process the frangipani is dipped in water and flicked three times, this increases the potency of the desire through the medium of that water, whether it be positive or negative.

If the practitioner wishes to anchor the energy of the frangipani within close proximity, they will light incense. To further bolster the circumstance, portions of rice or fruit can be laid at the site.

A lot of communities believe that the spirits in the area will be drawn to this place of worship in response to this gesture, but this is actually not the case. The spirit of the land - in terms of the ants, the birds, the bacteria - will absorb the desire and will then transport that intention to their natural resting places.

Thus the intent will be carried by these living beings to the four corners of the property. These insects and animals then become - through long term infusion of one's intent - unwitting allies to the practitioner. Their living fluids will resonate with the intention of the one who wields the magic.

This may seem interesting and absorbing, and a person may seek to obtain power this way. I was asked whether it is wise to tell the mechanisms behind techniques that can be so easily misapplied.

The reason I have displayed a portion of this information is to allow the seer to see that the old ways obtain the vibratory essence of their surroundings, which is possession at the deepest level imaginable.

What one must realize is that seeking this type of power is so detrimental, for what you covet eventually gains enough power through its own awareness to obtain and trap you within your own machinations; through mirrored, symbiotic intention.

What is echoed back ultimately is the sum total of everything outlaid. If this is not enough to deter the practice of black magic, then there is nothing more to be said.

There is another plant called daytura. I won't explain how to use this plant. Even speaking its name is dangerous enough. The daytura, if placed on a property, will absorb and reflect back the intentions of those that abide there. This plant magnifies control to such a degree that those who have weaknesses in this area are affected by the fibrous webs that this plant emanates.

I knew of one of these plants that was around eight years old, which had established itself so strongly on my friend's property that when the workers passed by, it pulled on their hair as if it was grabbing them.

That daytura instilled so much fear that they would give it a wide berth. It had so much power that it disrupted all the water that came into the property, resulting in taps not turning on and pipes leaking randomly throughout the vicinity.

The story goes with black magic that the stronger the power, the greater the loss of control of water is experienced in the area.

So be aware if you lose control of the water on your property that someone may be practicing black magic upon you. But this is not the point I wanted to make.

What I am getting to here is that, unlike the frangipani, the daytura has its own voice and its own intentions, and will endeavor to entrap and ensnare every being that is in it's vicinity, against their will. She is very dangerous and, like a female jackal, has mock genitals – a female and a male part to her.

A jackal displays these mock genitals to fool and coerce. Such is also the nature of this plant. Thus the coercive characteristics of the daytura and the jackal are unmasked by virtue of the fact that they each display something that appears to be what it is not, and by the time the warrior discovers that they have been tricked, it is too late.

When you intend with the frangipani negative or positive desires, whether you perceive yourself to be *black* or *white*, realize that you are relegating your consciousness to be entrapped; not only by your original desire but also via the fact that your environment will intend back to you who you are, making it more difficult to break your mirrored self reflection.

So *white*, when practiced with ignorance of consequences, is *black*, and for those who practice *black*, *white* is simply something to contend with. It ultimately is dualistic and futile to see anything from these two perspectives. Intend to be neither one, and allow the world around you to unravel you as you unravel it. Thus the middle way is revealed.

Technique 17:
Flower Gazing two

This technique is similar to *Flower Gazing One*, but the way the frangipanis are held in the container is different. The stand and backdrop are the same. Not using water makes this practice more potent in terms of having the capacity to see the blue.

Prepare:

- Several large bunches of frangipanis
- A deep wooden bowl
- Five or six tea-light candles
- Stand and backdrop

The tea light candles are placed in the bottom of the wooden bowl. The frangipanis are gathered in small bunches leaning outwards over the rim of the bowl so they form a glowing dome over the edge of the bowl. The shape of the bowl has to accommodate this and must be deep enough that the flames do not burn the petals.

This technique does not use water. It is a very powerful practice and it is of utmost importance that you never rotate your gaze in an anti-clockwise direction. The gazing is performed as in *Flower Gazing One*, rotating through the quadrants in a clockwise motion.

Technique 18:
Rainbow Gazing

Here I am including this gazing practice that was taught to one of my students, Ben Chandler, in dreaming, as he recounts in his story.

Last night I dreamed there was a rainbow gazing technique in the third eye book. It consisted of hard gazing at a rainbow, then closing the eyes and locating the subtle energetic imprint of the rainbow behind the closed eyes, visualizing it as though it was still there, then watching and breathing as the subtle imprint fades and vanishes.

At that point there was a kind of suction, void-type feeling of release, which I knew to be externalizing internal imagery and facilitating emptiness.

I have done this technique once before, not knowing where it came from. It was very subtle and delicate and silent. Since then I have been seeing rainbow inflections of energy that are very beautiful and heart opening.

In the dream I had never done the technique before and Lujan was teaching it to me. I knew it was 'in the book'. Maybe I had been remembering the future when I first did it a few months ago? A mystery...

In Bali I saw profound rainbow energy around Lujan at one point... It's impossible to describe, so beautiful! In the dream Lujan was guiding me to gaze at the rainbow for only short periods then close the eyes, release the vision and then I was for a moment suspended in emptiness without dream.

When the dream construct appeared again he would get me to immediately gaze again for a short while, then repeat the process multiple times. The rapid repetition between emptiness *and the technique felt like it was giving a very subtle and delicate part of my awareness a workout. It felt like flapping the butterfly wings of perception.*

Notes on *Rainbow Gazing*: This works with any refracted light, such as glass or crystal, not only rainbows.

Epilogue

It would be advisable to read this book and *The Art of Stalking Parallel Perception* several times, until you realize the multilateral points of reference that are embedded within each.

The interlinking aspects that are not immediately obvious will reveal themselves over time as abstract units of information that become available as one's attention becomes fluidly dimensionalized. You will begin to understand what is veiled, in terms of your consciousness traversing the delicate layers of third eye perception.

When performing all the techniques in this book you may

EPILOGUE

find that you will continue to skim through observance of your circumstance; recognizing the social nuances, yet not being involved through that recognition. This will transform your perception to be in a perpetual state of recapitulation.

You are witnessing that which unfolds as if it was at the moment of your death. Your right eye's social functioning has now been slowed down so dramatically that your left eye capacity to absorb has sped up, enlivening your body consciousness to recognize what it could not perceive previously. Wait patiently for your third eye functioning to open completely.

You will find that you will not, by virtue of this process, be interested in what you were before. Wait for your new self to arrive.

The techniques will eventually terminate the repetitive visual imagery that is normally internally generated and replace it with the origin of oneself: Nothing. Thus availing one to the natural spontaneity of our capacity to receive the random signals form the universe at large, which encompasses all variables.

EPILOGUE

The intent behind this book is to gear the seer towards freedom, towards the heart and away from control and stalking as a governing force. I hope that all that engage with these teachings have by this stage embraced this important step for humankind and no longer have any desire to dominate or manipulate others.

Not only this, the practices I have shared here will allow eternity to reflect back at the gazer their own intent. Again I reiterate the need to use these methods wisely, to embrace freedom and allow eternity to be your guide.

Endeavour to witness and not control the folly that arises. Learn to recognize what is seeking you. This will require you to drop the burden of agenda so as to receive the subtleties of that which you will learn to see.

Everything witnessed will ultimately be influenced by the insertion of your awareness. Your path will be self determined, guided by your own sovereignty.

For information regarding workshops and private

tuition with Lujan Matus please visit:

www.parallelperception.com

Printed in Great Britain
by Amazon